ANXIETY & PANIC and how to manage it by yourself

CHAPTER ONE

Quick Help

Firstly I am glad you made it here!
I believe many writers would put this part at the end of the
book, so you go through it all, but I'm sure you will anyway.
I did write this book to help and I know how panic works,
when you need help you don't have time to go through
100+ pages to collect the piece of information you need in
that moment! To overcome panic and anxiety is a recipe
with a lot of different ingredients but is flexible so that the
end result is what you want and what is best for you not
just what a book tells you to do. The first thing is to
embrace and accept it. The second is changing your
lifestyle. The changes you have to make are simple. Step
by step, you will learn how to deal with this thing that I am
sure makes your life somewhat bitter right now. Please
don't say "never" or "I can't" for a particular method; just go
and do it! Work with me here as I am trying to help you
right now. When you say to yourself 'oh, I can't do this' that
is all about saving yourself from some work, trouble or
inconvenience, but there is simply no such a thing as you
cannot in our situation. This is all a leap of faith. Bear with
me in this, please, as I'm committed to your well-being. I

was suffering from anxiety for way too long to let other people around me go through the same struggle as myself.

Please hear me out on this because I went through the same thing and slowly realized how it works and the factors that cause it. What are those slight differences that you make in your life as step by step you get closer to the point when you have a panic or anxiety attack?
We will reverse-engineer the process to get out of this cycle.

The main factors I was talking about are sleeping, behaviour before sleeping, morning routine and the things you do and think during the day. There are other factors too but I would instead call them triggers as they trigger you or make your anxiety worse.
 I'll go over them with you step by step. You don't have to change them overnight. Change always takes time. Lastly, I will tell you tips and tricks to make it easier to look forward on your path instead of going back. It is very important during this time to be consistent even if you feel like no changes are happening.
Professionals are still not precisely sure how anxiety and panic develop, but what they know is that the part of your brain responsible for the fight or flight response is overactive. When you get your trigger, like somebody is rude to you or you feel stuck in a situation, your body starts to produce adrenalin like crazy because your brain wants to protect you from any harm that comes your way.
We could call it a minor mistake as your brain becomes overprotective in situations when you do not need it to.
First things first, you don't need to fight it. At first it is perfectly normal to fight it but it is the same as when you try to force yourself to sleep—not going to work.
What you can do sounds pretty controversial. Simply say to yourself or 'to the panic': "All alright then, show me your worst! C'mon, I want to see what you can do". I encourage you to try and trigger the panic, what is the worst that's going to happen?

The panic will slowly fade away in the same manner as in the forced sleep example. Panic just won't work in this case. Sounds too unsophisticated a solution to work? It's just the way
to stop it.
You will still feel the vast amount of adrenalin in your body for a while which will feel like the panic is lurking in the background, waiting for the opportunity to catch you off-guard. It is quite the opposite. Once you have overcome the panic itself you need to turn your face towards some good old positivity. Your body needs some time to break down the adrenaline. I suppose if you feel you have breathing problems, you might do something other than breathing exercises, as they could make this more complicated. You may need a different kind of solution. What is very helpful is to find something you can play with, like a stress ball, a Rubik's cube or for some people simply staring through a window and looking at nature. I prefer the fidget cube, which fits in your palm and is full of buttons, drives your tension away very easily.
If you do not have breathing difficulties then you need to sit down and interlock your fingers comfortably, then rest them on your lap, close your eyes, and picture in front of you empty darkness, then imagine a nice big fluffy lavender coloured feather which is carelessly floating in the air. As it slowly descends, you take a deep breath through your nose, keep it in for a few seconds, then slowly exhale through your mouth. While you empty your lungs, the feather gently flies upwards to just above your eye line. You need to keep breathing to keep the feather floating. Do this exercise for a good 5 minutes and you will surely be over the hard part.
What you don't need is to repeat to yourself that you need to distract yourself. It would result in you falling back right into your previous state of nervousness for no apparent reason. You are already over that; keep going towards peacefulness.
You'll need to do it every time, whenever panic comes. Now that you know you can trigger the panic response

and slowly get better, you need to look at what triggers
your panic.
Panic won't just go away after you win once. I was
struggling with it for eight years before I figured it out. Try
not to think of it as an enemy because it's not a shadow or
some evil spirit that's not letting you be happy. It's all you!
You may feel that people or other things in your
environment are responsible for it, but it is all in your head.
As we look over the different people, many other things
cause it or make it worse, I will list the most common ones:
-Feeling of being trapped in a situation like being at the
shop in the line, sitting in traffic, in the elevator, on the bus
or the subway, in a big crowd
-A lack of breath after running, climbing stairs, being sick
or throat problems
-Strong smells
-Being dehydrated
-Feeling jumpy after too much coffee or tea
-Thinking of the future
-Winding up yourself over past conversations or arguments
-Being stuck somewhere and can't get to the toilet.
I have to tell you, I had it all and many times I felt the need
to cry at home after I went through a scenario. I just want
to live everyday life and want to be just like everybody
else.

You can do the absolute best thing without taking medicine
(although if you do, please contact a health care
professional before starting or stopping taking any
medication), you need to put the right habits together. If
you have anxiety, panic, or depression, you are doing
something wrong, like all of us do sometimes. When those
actions become habits, these will result in this complex
web of difficulties.
We will start with the sleeping part of it.
Sometimes I believe all of us who are in need of this book
had the feeling right after waking up that this day was
going to be wrong, you predict the whole day, what you

will have to do, how long your commute will be. Even before that you have the thought in the back of your head:
-"I can't do this."
-"It's too much for me."
-"I want to quit."
These thoughts especially come from bad experiences as you were anxious or kind of "jumpy" the day before. You think 'it's going to happen again'. If it's going to be like that, it's all going to be up to you and how you react to it. You need to embrace that horrible feeling and reassure yourself that it is all going to be okay. Panic cannot harm you!
The next important step will be how to start your morning to reduce this overactive instinct? Well, it is pretty simple. For the first 30 minutes of your day you need to stay away from your phone. Answering your messages as the first thing after waking up will change your reaction to the stress because you are already looking out for somebody's needs as you want to give them a reply. Barely any message would be of such grave importance that it cannot wait 30 minutes in the morning. If you do have important messages that require immediate attention in the mornings then let people know that you are trying to change your morning routine so they will know that you didn't ignore them, just that you need your morning to wake up fully. I will tell you how I start my morning casually to reduce the stress factors or triggers.
No coffee until 9 a.m. (if you wake up at nine, then push it at least an hour from the point you are awake)
Your body needs to do its work, like finishing digesting your dinner etc. You don't want to give it more things to deal with. Also, caffeine right after waking up makes anxiety worse. Then I drink 1liter of water, or if I'm going to travel considerable distances, just half a litre. Your brain functions better if you hydrate yourself sufficiently. The morning toilet routine will get back to normal in a little while if the coffee were your helper in this case.
Prepare yourself for the day with healthy thoughts. It sounds plain and simple, but it does start your day right.

What I mean by healthy ideas can really be anything. Pick
something that makes you happy, for example:
- It is a new day to create something
- To work on yourself
- To meet with people who you care about
- Do a favour for yourself by appreciating something that
  you like in you or about you
During the day, keep up your excellent work on yourself.
You don't have to concentrate on panic before you get to
that point. It's going to be in the back of your head anyway.
From that point on, you realize that it can't possibly hurt
you, these are just thoughts from your brain as it's trying to
protect you from harm. You will be in control of your day,
and even if people are not friendly to you or if the task you
are working on is rather depressing, it will get easier to
handle, and eventually the panic will fade away. The next
things to change are your evening eating habits and your
sleeping habits. Do not eat before sleep, allow at least 1.5
but better if it's 2 hours between eating and sleeping.
Going to bed with an empty stomach will give your body
the luxury of a routine and a rejuvenating night's sleep.
You need to develop a pre-sleep 'ritual', this should consist
of keeping yourself away from your phone, social media,
films, and every light source that would interrupt your
sleeping mind. When you lay your head to rest, your body
requires one thing. Which is to RELAX. Anything else is
just in the way of your progress in the way to get over
anxiety.

Do not keep yourself awake on purpose! What I mean by
that is when your life is all about work and a very moderate
amount of 'me' time at your disposal, you will find yourself
staying up late. In psychology this is referred to as
'Revenge bedtime procrastination' as you spend too much
time working on projects and at work in general, you arrive
home late, and you only have a few hours for yourself and
many times, even then you still need to do your chores at
home (laundry, dishes, cleaning, etc.), so you

subconsciously feel the need to take back control because you do want to spend some time with yourself and with activities that make you happy. When this is happening, you would like to use the most time you can squeeze out from the remaining hours of the day, and you may even calculate how many hours you can safely use to do your hobbies, watch films or series or play games. It is wrong! By depriving your sleep to spend more time for yourself, you cut your bedtime hours which will cause your mind to be on alert. Why? Because when your sleep schedule is interrupted your brain will notice it, and by instinct, it will keep the mind on its toes. In nature, usually, when sleep is interrupted, it is happening because of environmental changes and your mind registers these as threats. Let's say, for example you and your friends go camping and you are all sleeping in tents out in the forest. You are sleeping deeply, and then suddenly a branch breaks somewhere outside the tent. Your immediate reaction would be to wake up and be on the alert with adrenaline pumping in your veins, in your head you are already considering all possible scenarios; what was that? An animal? Someone walking around your camp? You'd be frightened probably. The same thing is going on when you keep messing up your sleep. Your mind will constantly calculate the threats and dangers around you because you slowly but surely create the same kind of environment for yourself as in the example. What you want to do is try to go to sleep at the same time every night and wake up at the same time every morning. I wake up every single day at 6 a.m., even on weekends, even during holidays, even at Christmas, because this is what works. It will gradually reduce the exhaustion that you would get by waking up at different times every day. If something unexpected happens, let's say somebody calls you in the middle of the night needing your help, you won't freak out because your body and mind are used to the nice consistent sleeping schedule, and one night is not going to turn that upside down. So please keep your bedtime nicely organized.

From that first day of your new schedule the trick is to keep it up so the next day repeat this circle of good sleep, good thoughts and to do a favor for your body in the morning and at night.
In the next part, we are coming back to what to do during the day?
You will see no instant solution for panic and anxiety, but progress, and as in every progress, sometimes there will be a few setbacks. If panic, fear, or depression is not overcome during the day, do not blame yourself for it. Change always takes time, and you have to be accepting and kind to yourself. I ask you to stick to these new habits even if they feel somewhat uncomfortable at the beginning. I remember when I started, and I always wanted a midnight snack or the morning coffee. After you put those things on a scale of importance, which is more beneficial for you? The rational answer is always going to be and is supposed to be your well-being!
To live without panic must be your number one priority because the more you sit on the problem the worse it's going to get. NEVER stop your new way of thinking and doing because it will go back to how it was before or even worse.

So if it's this simple, why are we not working on it?
Well, as always, there is no simple answer to it. The one thing I would blame for it is learned helplessness.
Learned helplessness is the mental state where an organism is forced to bear aversive stimulus or stimuli that are painful or otherwise unpleasant and becomes unable or unwilling to avoid subsequent encounters with those stimuli, even if they are escapable. I presume this is because the entity has learned that it cannot control the situation. So, in conclusion, when you did get into this situation, you didn't know what to do and just let it happen, as most of us do. Nobody was there to explain to you that "Hey, it's easier than you think; you just need to follow the

right steps." This is why I am here! You can control it! I believe in you with every cell in my body, and I know you feel there is an escape from this! There is an end to it, and it's not going to mean your end, only the anxiety, the end is to befriend it. Yes, I do view it like this sometimes. My slightly anxious friend was sitting on my shoulder to scare me from life. There is no such thing, but it was funnier to look at it like this for me.

I've had enough of avoiding trips, holidays, family activities, time with friends, restaurants, etc. Because this is what anxiety does, it restricts you from doing things that otherwise would be entirely normal. This is why it is a MUST to get over it as quickly as possible. You want life! You want to do things that make you happy!

Chapter 2 - Healthy thoughts

THE FIRST RULE:

In every moment of our life we evaluate ourselves and what we experience but our assessment of the situation is not always correct.

For example, we see a danger where there is none or exaggerate the extent of the threat and we underestimate or overestimate our coping options.

We see ourselves negatively and thereby weaken our self-esteem. We exaggerate the extent of a mistake or view a criticism as a devastating disaster. So our thinking is flawed. The consequences of our thinking errors are that we feel, for example, worse than they should be in the relevant situations.

We are afraid when there is no danger. We avoid situations or escape from problems that are not dangerous. We numb our negative feelings with addictive substances where there is no reason for these feelings.

We feel hurt and offended when someone else gives us their opinion. We feel hopeless even though there are solutions to our problems. We feel inferior even though we are lovable. So it is beneficial for us to make sure that our thinking is appropriate to the situation.

Healthy thinking corresponds to the facts.

Healthy thinking helps us feel and act the way we want to.

Conversely the hallmarks of faulty or inappropriate thinking looks like this:

-I don't deserve any better

-I'm fine as I am, it's the world that's broken

-Tomorrow's problem

-Why would I change when everybody else just wants to hold me back

-They are judging me

-I am a failure

-Nothing I do is good enough

A bad review is not based on facts but on our opinion or just guesswork.

Faulty thinking causes negative feelings and prevents us from feeling and acting the way we want to.

You can find out what thoughts are inappropriate for yourself by applying the two healthy thinking questions to your thoughts.

1. "Does my thought correspond to the facts?"
2. "Does my thought help me feel and act the way I want to?"

If you answer no to both questions you have found that your thinking is not appropriate to the situation and it does not help you achieve your goal, ask yourself the question.

'How should I think,feel and act to get the result I want?'

With the help of this question, you will find helpful thoughts that are appropriate to the situation. Sometimes we have a hard time doing this because we are convinced of our negative thoughts and have been thinking about them for a long time.

We can then look at other people who do not have this problem, or have already overcome it, as role models and ask how they assess the situation.

So to summarise the first rule of healthy thinking is that a healthy review is factual.

'it's not what happens to you, but how you react to it that matters' said the Greek philosopher Epictetus.

The importance you attach to something determines how you feel. It is always your personal views of reality that get you into trouble. If you always see things as they are, you will have no problems.

If you watch a cat play with a mouse for a while and then finally kill it, and you say "The cat is playing a cruel game" that is not a fact! The behavior of the cat is not cruel. You are expressing your opinion about a point. The cat is just doing what all cats do. It follows its instinct. The cat's behavior is neither good nor bad.

When you say "This is a boring Sunday" you're expressing your opinion about the day. The day as such is neither boring nor exciting.

If you say someone behaves badly, that is your opinion. They have a specific idea of what good and bad behavior looks like and judge others' behavior. However, your theory of what good and bad behaviors are would not necessarily be your own view but you may have adopted or inherited those views from your parents, siblings, those close to you or even the media.

Many people may share your opinion, but that doesn't change the fact that behavior is basically neither good nor bad.

Whenever you experience feelings that paralyze you and prevent you from living the way you want, your views are inconsistent with reality.

You see yourself and things through attitude glasses that distort reality. If you want to avoid or overcome feelings of unhappiness, fear, despair and anger, you need to base your thinking on the facts. Whenever you feel worse than you should ask yourself the following questions:

'Is my thought correct?'

'Is that true, or is it just my personal opinion?'

'Is there any evidence that it is a fact?'

In response to the question: 'Is my thought correct?' you need to be honest with yourself and really consider the question.

If you answer "No" to the question then it shows that you have exaggerated. You may have exaggerated the matter and made it worse than it is and since your thoughts determine your feelings, you also may have negative feelings or feelings worse than are appropriate for the situation.

THE SECOND RULE:

The second rule of healthy thinking is that healthy thinking helps you feel and act the way you want.

The most common reason people go into therapy or change their lives is that they don't feel the way they want to feel.

Like physical pain, negative feelings are a warning sign. While physical pain tells you that something is not working correctly in your body, negative feelings are an indication that you are evaluating something negatively.

If you consider yourself a failure or consider yourself inferior, it is perfectly normal to feel depressed and destructive. If you were in good spirits with such negative thoughts, that would be a sure sign that something is wrong with your brain. As long as you feel bad about such negative thoughts, you are perfectly healthy and normal.

But negative thoughts also prevent you from behaving the way you want. They lead to the fact that you might say "yes" when you want to say "no" or that you do not speak your mind or do not express your wishes because you fear that you will be rejected or laughed at.

Another effect of negative thinking can be that you don't do what you feel like doing because you are afraid of being criticized by others and that you cannot get your way. Negative thoughts also make it difficult for you to dare to try new things or live peacefully with those around you.

If you want to feel better about yourself and do more of what you think is right and good you need to change the way you think. Ask yourself "Does the thought of it help me feel and act the way I want me to?"

If the answer is 'no', then get that thought out of your head.

However, it is not enough to get a negative or exaggerated thought out of your head; you still need an alternative thought process to perceive things in a healthy way. You are looking for a positive, helpful view by asking, **"How should I think to feel and act the way I want to?"**

Before you can answer the question, you need to be clear about what goal you are trying to achieve. In doing so you should have in mind what you want to achieve and what consequences this could have in your environment. You should not choose goals that harm others or cause unwanted conflicts with them.

If you have found a suitable answer to this question then replace the negative thought with this more positive or realistic thought - whenever you think of it. This new helpful thought is also the basis for imagination exercises.

Healthy thinking does not mean thinking positively all the time. We cannot and do not have to see every situation positively.

There are occasions when it is appropriate to be concerned, sad, worried or disappointed, such as when our partner has left us, we have lost our job or have been given a severe diagnosis.

When I try to evaluate everything positively is not helpful. First, I think I was unlikely to succeed. Second, a positive evaluation does not help to change situations that we could change in our favor.

Persuading yourself that you will find your ideal partner or get the job of your dreams can lead to great disappointment.

But it is also not helpful to see everything negatively because then fear, frustration, sadness and anger are our constant companions. Persuading yourself that you will never get a partner or a job again would do us little good.

As long as we have not made serious efforts to change our situation then these thoughts are only a guess. For example a helpful attitude could be: "I will do everything to find a partner or a job. I have enough to offer."

Healthy thinking means thinking "appropriate to the situation." We do not underestimate our ability to influence, but neither do we overestimate them.

Living in the here and now - the journey is the goal

I grew up believing that the essential things in my life will happen in the future. So it's no wonder that, as an adult, I have entirely forgotten what it means to live in the here and now. But with that missing I never forget the essential prerequisite for being happy.

As children, we are taught to study so that we can get a good job later in life. Leading on from that view, throughout my life I have completed different internships and learnt two foreign languages to have better job prospects further down the line.

As I was starting in my career, I was told to work hard and work overtime to get promoted later.

And so the carousel keeps turning, and I kept chasing goals that I assume will contribute to my happiness.

Sure, it feels good to achieve these goals. But this feeling of what we mistakenly think is happiness never lasts long. Because now the next goal has to be completed. And again, we postpone the satisfaction of our needs into a hypothetical ideal future.

"I'll be happy once I've passed this exam" says the student, who has locked himself in his room for months and can no longer even notice whether the sun is shining or not.

 "I don't have time to look after the children now. But once I have the promotion in my pocket, everything will be different" says the workaholic, who has neither heard the first words nor seen the first steps of their children.

And who has not said: "I will start learning languages when ...".

'The journey does not matter, all that matters is the goal itself the way there is irrelevant'. That is the view of our western society today, which does not allow for the appreciation and significance or importance of the journey. How much we have changed in this regard can be seen from the word amateur.

The word amateur comes from the Latin "Amare, "which means "to love." So an amateur is a person who loves what they do.

Nowadays, the term is used disparagingly, denoting people who don't do something as well as "real" professionals.

So while the focus was historically on the experience, today it is only on the result. It has become irrelevant whether someone likes to do something or not. The only important thing is what comes out of it in the end.

So, in the past few centuries, we were trained to focus on our results and goals but have forgotten to appreciate our present.

This is precisely how we forfeit our chance of absolute satisfaction.

Try to make your everyday life as satisfying as possible so that you can draw joy from every single moment.

And the next time you catch yourself thinking, "so that I can later ..." say to yourself '**STOP**', take a deep breath and concentrate on the here and now.

Then it is no longer necessary to always subordinate your present to your future and struggle every day to achieve goals that are further and further removed into the future.

Chapter 3

Learning to be grateful

Learning to be more grateful - this is not only the noblest way to happiness and contentment but by becoming more appreciative it is the perfect antidote to frustration, envy, and anger. Gratitude is what we long for the most, recognition and appreciation for what has been achieved, a simple "thank you" for a good, generous deed. Writers, philosophers, and grandmothers rightly urge us to be grateful regularly, it is an essential key to a successful and fulfilling life. Why is gratitude so important and how you can learn and express it?

Gratitude is more than a "thank you" because someone did us a favor. To be grateful is an attitude. An attitude to life. "Gratitude is the feeling of astonishment, of being thankful and the celebration of life," says Robert Emmons one of the luminaries in gratitude research. Behind this is deeply felt appreciation and deep appreciation for a condition or care. Or as a quote from Jean-Baptiste Massillon says: "Gratitude is the memory of the heart."

Even the joy of the little things in life has been proven to lead to more happiness. Whoever establishes a grateful attitude in his life gives himself time to pause for spiritual rest and reflection. Gratitude is like taking a deep breath: We look at our life and recognize its true worth. Ask yourself what you can be thankful for! You are sure to find more than in the following list:

- The beauty of a sunrise
- The love of family
- For my health
- For the chef who prepared my meal

The things that you are thankful for do not have to be the 'big' things in life, it could be something as small as an appreciative smile.

In science and psychology, a grateful attitude has long been referred to as an "impact-intensive attitude to life".

Numerous studies demonstrate the positive effect of gratitude on the brain, health, and life satisfaction. Grateful people are more optimistic, happier, empathetic, fitter, and more resilient than others.

Examples from psychology and medical research:

Gratitude makes you happy - Robert Emmons and Michael McCullough.

For this experiment the researchers divided their test subjects into two groups: One group was given a few minutes to think about what they are grateful for in their lives. The others should just think of something. The researchers repeated the reflection exercises every week for ten weeks. Result: The thankful showed more motivation, greater optimism, even their health values and immune defence improved over the entire period. In short: the grateful thoughts made them happier and healthier.

Gratitude improves relationships. A psychology professor, Sara Algoe, from the University of North Carolina at Chapel Hill had new couples write a diary for two weeks in which they should record in the evening whether they had done something good for their partner that day, whether their partner had done them something good for them and how that made them feel. They then had to fill out how they now felt about the relationship Result: The couples noted that they not only recognized how good their partner was to them but overall they became more grateful for the cooperation and felt more connected to their partner.

Gratitude strengthens the heart. Studies carried out by researchers at UC San Diego School of Medicine even show that a grateful attitude reduces the risk of a heart attack. During medical examinations of people who state that they have a more grateful outlook on life their heart rate variability increased and cases of heart failure were rarer than in those people who did not share that same grateful attitude.

Gratitude helps with insomnia. This is the result of studies by Alex M. Wood of the University of Manchester (UK), a world-renowned gratitude researcher. His team determined that grateful people sleep better, deeper and fall asleep more easily. In short, compared to control groups, they suffered less from sleep disorders and were generally more productive.

Gratitude lowers stress. Gratitude makes you more resistant to stress. This was proven through research by Martin Seligman and Tracy Stephen from the University of Pennsylvania. Your - grateful - test subjects could reduce perceived stress and showed themselves to be more resistant to mental illnesses.

Gratitude helps fight depression. Being grateful has an enormous impact on the therapy of depression and anxiety disorders. In studies by researchers led by Prathik Kini from Indiana University, they had patients write thank you letters for 20 minutes three times a week. Three months later it became clear that the thank-you letters had activated numerous regions of the brain. The more often and more regularly the test subjects internalized gratitude, the more permanently it changed their brain and gave them a (new) positive attitude towards life.

Gratitude protects against temptation. Self-control or the ability to forego gratuities is a strong indicator of long-term success in life. Most people, however, prefer the immediate reward "Better the sparrow in hand than the pigeon on the roof ..." Instant pleasure instead of sensible foresight. According to Northeastern University studies, however, gratitude acts like a vaccine against all kinds of temptation. The grateful showed more patience and were willing to forgo instant rewards, which brought them higher profits in the long term.

Not every day is good, but every day has something good in it - you just have to recognize and want it. Gratitude can change our lives. Those who are grateful experience a deep feeling of happiness, satisfaction, and joy, and not just for a short time. Over time it becomes a state of mind. The overall favorable mood that creates gratitude leads to what is known as a "broad-and-built effect" as scientist Barbara Fredrickson calls it. In short, this means that lived appreciation always leads to other positive effects.

Based on all that we can safely state that gratitude can have the following positive impacts:

• We value our life more again. Especially the little things.

• We become more confident.

• We radiate more satisfaction and thus appear more attractive to others.

• We can resist temptation better because we need less.

• We react to changes with less stress.

• We have fewer fears.

- We see more opportunities and possibilities.

- We become more relaxed about crises and can cope with them more quickly.

- We become more resilient.

- We strengthen our well-being and self-esteem.

- We pave the way for a fulfilled life.

Lack of gratitude: Ingratitude is a career killer

Without gratitude, on the other hand, a flawed view often develops life - it mainly consists of gaps, missing things, emptiness. Anyone who perceives themself and their environment in this way can only become dissatisfied, envious, and unhappy. The grass is always greener on the other side for these people. Such ingratitude is dangerous! Goethe, a historic German poet, emphasized that he did not believe "that capable people would have been ungrateful." History proves him correct, it was not those who had a lot who were successful, but those who were grateful. Or as another quote says: "It is not the lucky ones who are grateful. It is grateful who are happy." No human being will be grateful for future successes if he cannot already be grateful for present ones.

Even more though ingratitude can mutate into a career killer. Ingratitude is a lack of gratitude and a lack of appreciation for the support. For example, hiding the fact that others were involved. Forgetfulness weighs even more heavily, however. No one expects immediate consideration for a favor. Only those who forget this guilt are engaged in self-sabotage of the first order. Ingratitude is not a trivial

offense but a gross violation of a professional iron law...
'one hand washes the other'.

The 5-finger method: a thank you with every finger

Among the various tips and techniques for remembering
what to be thankful for, there is a wonderful one from
Elsbeth Martindale. The psychologist recommends: "If you
are dissatisfied again or need a motivational kick, just
count your fingers and remember beautiful, satisfying, and
encouraging things in your life." For example:

Thumbs up: Name something you are proud of. Make
yourself aware of your strengths and talents - and be
proud of yourself.

Index finger: Point to something beautiful in nature.
Discover something in your environment that inspires and
excites you.

Middle finger: What is the name of one thing you did for
another person that you feel good about? Think about who
you can repeat this with—for example, today.

Ring finger: Remember a time and a person whom you
love or have loved from the bottom of your heart, as well
as other people for whom you have deep feelings.

Little finger: What is one thing that you are deeply grateful
for in your life?

The hand idea has charm because, firstly, it is catchy and,
secondly, it can be repeated at any time. "Anyone who
always wants the whole cake to themselves will only get a
stomach ache from it" is a lovely saying and quote. The

selfless act and a "thank you," on the other hand, pay off in the long term.

For many years I struggled with guilt because I couldn't feel the feeling of gratitude. I could look around, and with my mind, I could tell myself that I had every reason to be grateful. I just wasn't able to feel that feeling often. There always had to be something outside to activate the surface.

For a long time, I thought I was an apathetic, ungrateful person until I discovered that gratitude is also a muscle that needs training.

My gratitude muscle was so slack and underdeveloped because I was so busy feeling sorry for myself, lingering in my victim role, and just focusing on what I was missing and what I didn't have that I had forgotten entirely to train it. If there is one thing our ego cannot, it is to be thankful.

The ego always wants to have, never to give, and is therefore in direct opposition to gratitude.

I realized that I had to build a routine - similar to having to retrain a weak back or broken leg. I slowly built up a morning and evening routine. It only takes a few minutes, but this routine has changed my life significantly, for every day and for my ability to be grateful.

When I wake up in the morning, the first thing I do is to say 'thank you' to myself. I say 'thank you' while I'm still in bed.

I thank you for the day, for life, and for what was and what is to come. I remember who I am - that I am not a body but a soul with a purpose. I give thanks for my soul, which is very simple: giving and receiving love and being happy. When I am so glad, I send out a vibration that causes the universe to send even more joy in my direction. On the other hand, if I'm sad and worried all the time, I get more of it. It's just the law of attraction that goes into effect. You get more of what you send out; like attracts like.

I have already connected to the universe and the loving energy in and around me in the morning. If you cannot connect with the universe, start by clicking with reality, with the day about to begin, and walk consciously into the day with the right energy, intent, and joy. Remember that joy is a conscious choice that we make.

In the end we can only get what we are ready to give. So, if you want unconditional love or something else in your life, look carefully to see if that is what you are giving to others. The joy comes from within.

Be aware of everything that you already have in your life every day, not what you do not have or what you lack. Just observe what you already have and what you are grateful for. Every evening write a list of at least five things that you were thankful for during the day. Or look inside yourself and go through the things you were grateful for that day, one at a time.

If you want to train your gratitude muscle, using the five finger method. It will help you prepare your gratitude and remind you to appreciate things in your daily life. Every day the technique will lead you to grateful thoughts.

CHAPTER 4:

Self-appreciation and loving yourself

We often do not even notice how much we do in everyday life. Countless tasks and the daily stress we are exposed to leave us no time to perceive our surroundings correctly. Stop it! It is time to enjoy life by noticing the beauty of everyday things. Learn to appreciate the ordinary things in your life and be inspired by simple moments. You will see how your mood lifts instantly!

We must appreciate the pleasant moments in our life or we will miss them completely. Instead, we are always in a hurry and run from one thing to another. We always postpone our happiness because we often believe that it can only be achieved through the big things in life like professional success, wealth or a senior position. However, if we only focus on what remains to be done, the here and now usually falls short. Slow down and learn to appreciate the little joys in your life.

Most of us get annoyed when we can't find our favourite brand in the supermarket or when someone jostles us in line at the checkout. We get restless waiting for a pedestrian to cross the street or when something is holding us back at work. Why do we get so upset about little negative moments instead of enjoying the simple things we experience every day? Why can't we enjoy beautiful weather, a stranger's smile, a pleasant scent or just a hot cup of coffee while enjoying the view from the window?

It is usually the minor everyday events that make you the happiest! Do you not think? Think about it: what has been giving you pleasure lately? The day you got a promotion at work is unlikely to come to mind. Not even the moment you bought a new house. I often just remember the ordinary moments I enjoyed - whether it's a beautiful sunset, a relaxed picnic in the park or a friendly chat with my neighbour. It's the little things that I remember. The little moments in my life that sometimes pass by almost unnoticed, but that can mean a lot more than I would have thought. It's always amazing to me.

LEARN TO APPRECIATE THE LITTLE THINGS!

Be attentive and watch the world around you. Let smells and tastes affect you and positive memories from your childhood or youth will awaken. Think about all the beautiful moments in your life. Perhaps the scent of raspberries in your grandparents' garden comes to mind. Or the soft cheeks of your children when they were little. A fun evening with old friends where you spent hours talking about your school days. Do you remember that strict teacher who taught you? Or your first crush? Every life is made up of innumerable tiny details and it is up to you to enjoy and appreciate them.

You don't have to be a world champion, millionaire, or Nobel Laureate to enjoy life and learn to appreciate the little things. Lifelong happiness is found in the simplest things we see in our everyday lives. As the saying goes 'The best things in life are free!'

We like to compare ourselves to other people. In this comparison, those we compare ourselves to usually appear better than us. He can do it better; she looks better. Our inner voice usually finds something that others can do better, that others have that we don't.

There is so much that makes each of us unique, lovable, individual. We see it far too seldom or not at all.

Exercise 1: 'That's what I love about myself'

Find a place where you are comfortable. Then pick up a pen and a piece of paper.

On that piece of paper write down at least ten things you love about yourself.

Do not stop listing until you have at least 10 points; if you found ten things quickly, so much the better. Keep going with your list until you can't think of anything else.

Such a list could look like this:

1. What I love about myself is that I can laugh at myself.

2. I love my sense of humour.

3. I love my long hair.

4. I love my calm manner.

5. ...

It's not about listing who or what you love, just what you love about yourself. Then, if you can't think of anything else, put this list away somewhere easily accessible. You will find that just by keeping such a list will you become more aware of what else you love about yourself.

You may find it difficult to list things that you love about yourself. Many people find it much easier to list what they don't like about themselves.

If you have trouble doing this, ask yourself what people you trust, love, or appreciate about you. Or even better: ask these people directly, e.g. your partner, parents, etc. You will be amazed at their answers and learn a lot that makes you particularly lovable.

Exercise 2: 'I can'

Now let us go a step further. When comparing with others, we often see what we cannot do or do not have and then overlook our strengths. In any case, I think that many people are not aware or underestimate their own strengths; and that's a shame because if you know your strengths and talents, use them consciously, and maybe even use them in your job, things will be much easier for you. And the reward: numerous personal moments of success.

But how do you become aware of your strengths?

Self-reflection also helps to become aware of one's strengths and talents. Go back to your sheet of paper or notebook, where you have listed the things you love about yourself.

Now on the back of that list or on a new sheet, write down everything that you are particularly good at. The following example questions can help:

1. What have I always been good at school?

2. What am I particularly good at?

3. What have I often received praise and recognition for?

List as many traits and skills as you can think of. Again, ask people around you if you are unsure.

The same applies here: If you can't think of anything, it doesn't mean that you have found all your strengths and talents. With this list alone, your subconscious will repeatedly draw your attention to forces that you were not yet aware of.

My way to love yourself

The most stunning, all-changing, most beautiful time of my life was learning to love myself and thus love in general. I haven't had it that long, but I don't want to miss it any day of my life because it blooms and blooms and gives me joy and strength every day.

I was brought up on responsibility, the duty to others, and a distorted self-harming form of humility. Pretty much anything, just not self appreciation or a sense of self worth. Nobody in my family could demonstrate this to me; they didn't know how to love themselves.

I don't hold it against my family. It no longer hurts or restrains me. I have never questioned their love for me or thought that they deliberately wanted me to do the slightest bit of evil. On the contrary, I believe that they try wholeheartedly to protect me from pain, disappointment, and an evil, sorrowful life from their perspective. I think that their fear and worry drove them - for themselves and the people who mean a lot to them (as have I for most of my life).

Shared love begins with loving yourself.

A lot had to happen to me until I could finally understand that in order to deal with the anxiety and panic I had to change my way of thinking from the ground up. I had to keep adjusting my thinking until suddenly the anxious part of me was exposed and I could start to address the issues. The goal of this being that I would no longer be controlled by fear and through this I discovered that the first step to fixing yourself is to start learning to love yourself.

I have realized that I treat others like myself, whether I want to or not. And others treat ME as they do themselves.

LIKE yourself ...

Until I - and I am not a religious person - suddenly became aware that the bible says "love your neighbour as yourself", and not "love your neighbour more than yourself", or even "love your neighbour instead of yourself".

It is precisely the self-love and the self-confidence that results from it that generates inspiring, uplifting charity.

For me, it was a long, arduous and challenging path to this realization, which I would like to spare you from the rather long explanation. But I would like to give you some good news:

There is no substitute for loving yourself

The people in our immediate environment, who courageously trust themselves to do everything and openly love, respect and appreciate themselves, do not try to overshadow us. They invite us to step into the light with them.

They don't need others; they can enjoy them. They do not abuse others as substitutes for self-love or consolation; they do not hold others responsible for satisfying their own needs; they have something extraordinary to give away.

They do not judge others, do not slow them down, they do not allow themselves to be easily unsettled by others, they do not want to hurt or weaken others or intend to smack them with "I am better than you!" You don't need to be validated or uplifted by others.

Infect others with your own love

They just try to infect others with their love, to give them wings and to inspire them, to liberate and enrich them and to encourage them in their personal development, because what they have in common makes life far more fulfilling.

For me, these people are the most beautiful blossoms in life. I am so happy (and lucky) that I have a wonderful example of that love in my life and that I was able to get infected with this love at the moment when I needed it most. And now I very much wish to infect others with it.

Chapter 5

Things you should avoid if you have anxiety or panic disorder

Anxiety is a complex condition that cannot be resolved with a smile and a nod—telling us 'that everything is fine' does not help us. Worse, it gives us the impression that no one takes us seriously.

Most of the people I confide in about my struggles with anxiety disorder nod their heads and tell me that I will be fine. When I tell them "I'm sorry, but I feel very anxious today, can we postpone the meeting?" They smile and tell me that there is nothing to worry about and that I will realize that all is well as soon as I get out of bed. When I refuse to go bar crawling because I know that alcohol only exacerbates my anxiety, I am told: "Come on, let's have fun. Relax!"

At such times my heart beats so hard that I'm afraid everyone will see it thunder against my chest. But no. My head does not loop. I'm not squinting, and my knees aren't staggering to keep me from falling. I am not as pale as a sheet, and my eyes are not bloodshot.

There is no indication of any problem. My hair is clean, and my clothes are matching. I am awake, alive and breathing easily. So, everything is fine.

No.

This is the problem with anxiety disorders. I could not identify anything from the outside. No broken leg. No gaping head wound. No cuts or bruises. Quite simply, even though anxiety is not a physical handicap, it is nonetheless disabling.

So here are a few things I would like you to know about tackling anxiety.

Anxiety is not permanent.

There are days when I don't need to stop everything to catch my breath and calm down or grab a pill. I manage to smile and laugh. I tend to be productive, get to work, eat out for an evening, or see a movie with my friends. And believe me, I know how hard it is to understand why I'm fine one day when I can't get out of bed the next. It's like that.

This brings me to the next point:

It works in waves

Anxiety is weird. It lets me have fun for two days, and I tell myself that maybe it finally left me alone. And then, one morning, I wake up, unable to think because, for some reason, I don't know why but it's back. And there is nothing to do about it because I woke up feeling the pressure in my chest but then putting on false smiles pretending as if I were happy to find it again.

It can be downright crippling.

I don't know if this applies to everyone, but it is an essential aspect of my anxiety. When it hits me, it paralyzes me. I can get up and do what I have to do, but my mind is elsewhere, prisoner of the "demon" that has taken hold of me. I am obsessed with my inability to think, breathe, or feel. I let this feeling set in. I feel like my brain is paralyzed, like I am lost in limbo, with no door, window or emergency exit.

And the worst part about it is that I am entirely alone.

Anxiety can have terrible effects if you don't know how to deal with it. It may become too heavy for those closest to you to carry. If they get close enough to you to experience the effects of your anxiety, they may reach a saturation point where severing ties becomes necessary for their sanity. And it hurts like hell.

For people with panic and anxiety disorders, everyday life can be more complex than you imagine. They are confronted with the freezing fear of particular events, the creeping thought of a panic attack and the lingering physical symptoms.

And it can all be all the more difficult to live with when you have it—feeling that no one else understands how it feels.

Being anxious is not just being stressed.

When you tell someone you have anxiety disorders, their first reaction is to understand what you are going through (although stress and anxiety can be different for everyone). This expression of empathy is a natural reaction, but it is not always the most significant help, as people with anxiety disorders know how tiring it can be to overthink (but there's nothing you can do about it).

It's a vicious cycle: your thoughts become your fears, and your worries become your thoughts. However, being obsessed with it can have consequences, according to a study published in the journal 'PLOS One' researchers have found that brooding over negative thoughts is one of the biggest triggers of depression and anxiety. The psychological reaction to an event is even more critical than the event itself.

I would suggest seeking help if you are concerned about being too lost in the negative. These emotions that people with anxiety experience are real, they weren't created in your head.

Your phobia can be fun.

As many of us enjoy teasing people with phobias, for example, by showing a spider image to an individual with arachnophobia. Whether or not you intend to be cruel, I would suggest exploring your empathetic side before making a joke. Think about the fact that these fears, however irrational and difficult to understand, are very real to the person concerned. It is best to view people with courtesy and respect.

A stigma can be linked to treating emotional and mental disorders with medication – and those who go through medication to overcome their anxiety are likely to experience that feeling of embarrassment that comes with taking pills. As written by Tom Wootton (a speaker and author specializing in mental health) in his blog in Psychology Today he said that stigma is one more sign of the fear of uncertainty. "You can be afraid of a lot of things, but the worst fear is about what you don't know." he wrote. "The combination of fear and ignorance is so powerful that many people think fear is just another word for ignorance … But when you understand the fear and what role it does, it works in our case; we can turn it into a tool rather than letting it destroy us."

How do you recognize anxiety at night?

Unfortunately, there is no way to prevent an attack like this, but a few symptoms can tell you whether you had a panic attack in your sleep soon after you wake up. These would be, among others:

Increased heartbeat

Chest tightness

Shortness of breath

Hyperventilating

Sweating

Chills

If you have any of the above symptoms, it can be assumed that you experience typical anxiety states at night. Unfortunately, breathing problems can have more impact at night than during the day. Often this is noticeable with heavy and fast breathing.

However, if you prepare and inform yourself sufficiently beforehand, you can avoid panic in an emergency. Because if you know what to expect, you can react accordingly.

If you are unprepared, fear of anxiety at night alone can be a big problem for you. A sudden attack in particular can trigger panic fear.

Please do not confuse this with night terrors because these usually occur with nocturnal physical activity or sleepwalking. Treating night terrors is different from panic attacks.

What can be the cause?

The worst symptoms are breathing problems. The triggers can be very different. Heartburn or hyperventilating, for example, can contribute to this. People who have a problem with this may experience night-time anxiety more often.

Most people don't want to deal with their problems, even during the day. The result is that the panic attacks can hit even worse at night.

Many can breathe normally during sleep, but if there are breathing problems, the person concerned may hyperventilate even during sleep. This can also lead to a panic attack.

What if the symptoms appear regularly?

If you go through this more often, you have probably already been examined for a suspected heart attack. This is not uncommon, an anxiety attack at night has symptoms very similar to a heart attack and can easily be mistaken for one.

The pressure on the airways increases, which you shouldn't take lightly in the long run. Especially not if you have already experienced a situation like this several times.

Surprisingly, people with sleep apnea can go back to sleep after waking up at night. However, if anxiety disorders are the cause, the situation is very different.

It is best to go to a therapist, who will measure your bio- and neurofeedback, test your emotional body reactions, and support you.

What do bio and neurofeedback mean?

Your body gives measurable biofeedback. This is direct feedback from the body and includes reactions such as heightened pulse rate or blood pressure, sweating, breathing quickly, and more. Properly measuring these can show how exactly these reactions interact.

Neurofeedback on the other hand is where the reaction is purley neurological, for instance this can include a feeling of being followed, inability to focus, hyperactivity or anything else that is entirely internalised rather than physical.

A therapist can then train you specifically on what changes in your lifestyle or thought processes to improve your situation in order to overcome anxiety at night.

For example, during the therapy session brain waves (EEG) or heartbeat (EKG/ECG – these are both acronyms for Electrocardiogram so mean the same thing) are measured and displayed graphically on a computer. In this way, the therapist can identify the connections between individual reactions and feelings in order to help you get to the root cause of the issue.

In this way, they can give you the support and tools to get your anxiety under control at night on your own and show you the possibilities accordingly.

For this reason, bio and neurofeedback play a significant and vital role in this topic. This effectively treats fears and other mental illnesses. So far, biofeedback therapy has been particularly successful in treating tinnitus, pain disorders, the effects of stress, etc.

You can also measure your heartbeat from the comfort of your own home so that you can check it yourself. Various devices such as a mobile EKG measuring device for smartphones and smartwatches can be used to measure heart rate and you can experiment to find out what elevates it. If you are concerned, you can even email the data to your doctor.

"Fight" panic attacks and overcome fears.

You went to your family doctor and found out that you have a panic disorder. The symptoms are not coming from anything else. What now? You get rid of the anxiety attacks when you get rid of the fear of new anxiety attacks.

How do you teach yourself these thoughts? You can go to **psychotherapy;** the psychiatrist will practice the correct thought patterns with you. You may be given **antidepressants** for the first time.

Antidepressants and anti-anxiety drugs

These tablets can suppress anxiety attacks for a short time, but they can occasionally cause severe drowsiness. If you have agoraphobia with panic disorder, psychotherapy is your best choice.

Behavioural therapy can help with panic attacks and also help you to deal with phobias.

If you only have anxiety attacks and the occasional bout of fear and no other illnesses, **meditation** can certainly be an alternative. Get rid of stress where you can.

Think about what is worrying you. What problems can you solve quickly? Which can you let someone else solve?

A regular daily routine - the secret weapon against stress and anxiety

What is your day like, orderly or chaotic? **Irregular eating and sleeping times** can cause a lot of pressure on your body, and your brain too. You should, therefore, always get up at the same time. Eat at least three meals a day. Start with a hearty breakfast as soon as you get up.

Lunch and dinner should be at the same time whenever possible. If you are prone to hypoglycemia, plan small snacks between meals. Keep a calendar for your appointments and tasks. Don't put off anything; get everything done as soon as possible.

In this way, you avoid stress and worries, and the problems rarely occur. With a **regular daily routine** and good navigation through everyday life, you will have significantly fewer anxiety attacks than if you are living a hectic or chaotic lifestyle. Maybe the problem is completely solved.

Biofeedback: get to know your body

Anyone who has panic attacks no longer trusts their own body. As soon as your heart beats a little faster, you fear the next attack. Often there is even a perfectly normal and mundane reason for the increase in heart rate. For example, you've just climbed a flight of stairs or had one too many coffees - your heart must be beating faster! You can learn to trust your body and brain again and find your way back to a healthy state.

Again, **meditation** will help you. You can also have your **physical activity** measured or measure it yourself. Consciously experience your body's typical reactions: If you are excited or in motion, your breathing gets faster.

When you are relaxed, your heart and breath are calm. Soon you can be sure that your body will genuinely react, no matter where you are. That is to be done now.

Getting a grip on anxiety at night

The following tips will help you if you have been woken up at night again. In such a case, it is best to act immediately.

Tip 1: focus on your breathing

If you have been awakened at night by anxiety then your first priority must be to get control over your breathing, slow your breathing. Breathe deeply in through your nose and slowly out through your mouth. Feel your heartbeat and breathing return to normal. You will find that you will soon be better.

Tip 2: turn on the lights

If you have been awakened by anxiety at night, the best thing to do is turn on the lights. This gives you a feeling of security, and you can see that everything is fine around you. This method is better than rolling around in bed in the dark. You can also consider putting a lamp on a voice-controlled switch or a clapper so rather than scrabbling for a light switch, whilst in a state of panic and in the dark, you can clap or tell the light to turn on.

Tip 3: Talk to yourself

That might sound a little strange but talking to yourself calms you down in such a situation. Say something nice and remember it. This will stop you from hyperventilating, and your breathing will become calmer. A good book against fear and worries can also bring you new ideas. I also find rationalisation helps, so as you are talking to yourself remind yourself that the doors are all locked, the dog is asleep and nobody is about to kill you.

Refrain from any negative external input. Don't leave negative movies, books, and thoughts in your head. Replace them with content that adds value to your life.

Tip 4: do something relaxing

It is good to do something relaxing. Have some soothing caffeine free tea, do a yoga exercise, or take a hot bath. You can also use meditation apps to help with relaxation.

Tip 5: Eat a healthy diet

Eat a balanced and healthy diet to prevent anxiety at night. Under no circumstances should you go to bed on a full stomach. This can lead to heartburn, sleep problems, and bad dreams.

Many people suffer from anxiety because they do not have a healthy diet and consume too many unhealthy drinks. If possible, avoid caffeine, alcohol, sweets, chips, and the like. Smoking can also lead to anxiety. Instead, get in the habit of drinking a green smoothie in the morning.

Tip 6: do sport

Exercise can help you reduce stress and sleep better at night but make sure to leave at least a couple of hours between exercise and bed time. Sport also keeps you fit and healthy. If you exercise regularly, you will notice that tension, and thus certain feelings of anxiety can be reduced.

It also sets you free and distracts you from negative thoughts. Drivers, in particular, have no natural physical stress relief while driving. Therefore, stress is felt, but the movement that occurs naturally in response to stress is lacking, debilitating it.

Tip 7: Document your anxiety at night

While it may seem strange, documenting your panic attacks can help. You can then see if the intensity and frequency have become better or worse in the long run. You also create an awareness of your feelings.

This alone can, in some cases, eliminate anxiety at night.

Chapter 6

How yoga and other exercises

can reduce anxiety

Yoga for anxiety and panic attacks with three asanas -
body postures

How much easier and more worthwhile could everyday life
be if fear weren't constantly restricting and limiting you by
narrowing your options, for example stopping you from
going to the shops or even answering your front door. The
worry is capable of literally freezing a person and
rendering them incapable of action from one moment to
the next.

When we are afraid, our posture, our facial expressions,
and gestures change. Our voice takes on a different pitch,
and we move differently. These observable changes are
the physical reaction to the internal psychological
processes. Just as the psyche affects the body, the
conscious assumption of a particular physical position, as
practised in yoga, influences our psychological well-being.
As a result, we can control our psyche through the
conscious alignment of our body and can provide an
independent and purposeful influence. With normal
anxiety, we become more alert and active. If it gets out of
control, it robs us of the air to breathe and makes us
unable to act or react. The origin and development of fear
clearly express how the body and the psyche work
together as an inseparable unit.

Fear is nothing more than the physical indication of an
actual or suspected danger. The sympathetic nervous
system is overactive, and all psychophysiological
processes are going crazy. If we now consider that holding
a mobilizing yoga asana for a long time calms the
sympathetic nervous system, which maintains fear, and
activates the parasympathetic nervous system, which
alleviates it, the duration of the yoga asana for fear should
not be less than 30 seconds. Longer holding times of the

asana calm the system and give us back control over our emotions. The holding time is just one factor affecting the parasympathetic nervous system activated in acute anxiety. The pressure receptors can also explain the calming effect of yoga's physical postures on the psyche in the skin and by encouraging exhalation.

Marjarasana - the diagonal cat pose

Marjarasana, the cat pose, is an exercise that gently strengthens our brain and our mental and physical balance through concentration and focus. This asana requires intense attention and focus on an external object. The material balance can thus be better maintained. Marjarasana also combines two types of yoga exercises: postures that promote balance and activities that strengthen and tense the body. On the one hand, Marjarasana supports attention and balance through finding and maintaining physical equilibrium; on the other hand, this exercise teaches us that deep and regular breathing can alleviate uncomfortable physical conditions by consciously breathing into them, where fear is perceived in the body. This experience makes us more willing to accept our inner tension and anxiety during the exercise. Combining the balancing exercise with the practice of taking and bearing unpleasant things favours our handling of fear. The solid physical stress combined with a substantial concentration on an external object lets us forget our fear for a short time. The aspects of tension and relaxation also come into play here. After dissolving the asana, those affected feel deep relaxation through the previously felt muscular tension. Accepting and enduring unpleasant things helps us deal with fear. The solid physical stress combined with a substantial concentration on an external object lets us forget our fear for a short time. The aspects of tension and relaxation also come into play here.

The cat pose clearly shows us our physical and psychological limits. Therefore, a lot of patience is required at the beginning. However, our body's experience gradually adapts and changes to the new stress and strengthens our (self) confidence. We get the opportunity to learn from ourselves that patient practice, even with acute anxiety, leads to physical and psychological growth.

The improved physical coordination in Marjarasana goes hand in hand with a positive effect on the regions of our brains that are responsible for awareness, control, and emotion regulation.

Method:

1.   Get into the four-legged position, knees and palms flat on the floor. Make sure you have a straight back. Look straight ahead. Breathe in and out deeply and regularly

through your nose.

2.   While still on all fours, focus your gaze on an object outside. Once you have identified a fixation point for yourself, remain focused on it. At the same time, the next time you inhale, bring your right arm forward so that you are pointing away from you with your arm level with your chin. With the next inhalation, stretch your left leg backwards raising it up straight, following the line of your back with your toes extended. Your gaze is fixed on the previously determined object, and all your attention is focused. Hold this position for five to 30 breaths - depending on how long you can hold this position without overwhelming yourself.

3.   After practising the Cat Pose for five to 30 breaths, release the asana and sit back on your heels. Relax your spine and head while doing this. The arms remain loosened and stretched forward on the mat. This position is known as balasana, the child's or resting pose.

The child's pose is used to relax the body and feel the effects of Marjarasana deeply. If you have the feeling that you have recovered sufficiently, repeat the exercise as shown from step 1 with the other side of the body.

You will find out relatively quickly that this asana is quite physically demanding.

However, try to resist the impulse to stop the asana prematurely for as long as you can. Every new motivation and decision to remain in the asana and to accept the unpleasant physical tension creates an opposite impulse in

our organism. It strengthens the ability to control our actions and emotions.

Adho Mukha Svanasana - Downward Facing Dog

Another asana that can be used with acute anxiety that reduces the stress response in the body is the downward-facing dog. This asana helps alleviate the symptoms of anxiety mainly because the position of the body automatically reinforces the exhalation process. Increased exhalation, in turn, inhibits the sympathetic nervous system and the physical symptoms of stress it causes, such as sweating, tremors, increased heart rate, etc. For more extended periods (up to two minutes), it also activates and promotes the parasympathetic nervous system via the stretched muscles' receptors. This leads to a feeling of physical and mental relaxation. The trunk's lowering and stretching also favour cerebral blood flow and stimulate the core of the cardiovascular system (pulmonary circulation), which invigorates our brain. This asana not only helps to alleviate internal stress but also to relieve exhaustion.

Although Adho Mukha Svanasana promotes cerebral blood flow, it can also be used without problems and is harmless in those with high blood pressure.

In addition to the symptoms already mentioned, a significantly increased emotional stress level and fear also lead to muscular tension in the shoulders and neck. Because in Adho Mukha Svanasana, the sciatic nerve is activated by stretching the back, the stiffness and pain in the lumbar spine, ankles, and heels can be alleviated. Active relaxation of the cervical spine and stretching of the neck and shoulders also relieve stress-related complaints in these areas. The physical tension caused by fear subsides. The comprehensive effect becomes more intense, and relaxation is more significant with each execution. The best way to understand the pleasant impact is to experience it so now is a perfect opportunity for you to try the downward facing dog. Depending on the physical ability the holding time can vary between 30 seconds and several minutes.

Method:

1.   Get into a four-legged position with your feet and hands on the floor and legs and arms straight. Make sure you have a straight back. You are entirely focused and

attuned to your body. You breathe in and out deeply and regularly through your nose. If you stay in this position for a moment, you will again feel the contact points between the mat and your palms and the back of your feet.

2.   The next time you exhale, press your palms firmly into the ground, bring your buttocks up and stretch your legs as far as you can. Your gaze is still firmly directed forward. Now shift your entire body backwards so that your buttocks are the highest point of the angle. At the same

time, open your chest and bring both shoulder blades together.

Relax your head and neck by letting your head hang loosely between your elbows.

During Adho Mukha Svanasana, be careful not to tense your neck. This can quickly happen in this position, as we tend not to let go of the head and neck, especially at the beginning of the practice, and lift forward to look. It is essential to actively relax your upper back and cervical spine in this position and let your head hang loosely on. This is the only way to achieve the desired physical and psychological relaxation.

3.   Hold this position for five to 30 breaths. Continue to breathe deeply in through your nose and deeply and slowly back out through your mouth.

When the exercise is over, relax your body into the child's pose (balasana) and feel the asana's effects on the body and mind.

If it is easy for you to remain in the downward facing dog, it is advisable to hold the asana for up to two minutes and maximize the parasympathetic nervous system's effect.

The downward facing dog, in particular, can cause problems when you first begin to practice it. If the body is not used to this stress it isn't easy to relax in this position and to endure it. But if we repeat this exercise regularly our body adapts to the load and a physical sense of well-being, along with deep psychological relaxation is experienced. We link the positive physical and mental sensation that this asana gives us in our brain. This means that any other practice of Adho Mukha Svanasana leads to relaxation more quickly through this connection.

This exercise's effect on our body and our psychological wellbeing can also be increased by controlling breathing. If when you are practicing any asana you breath using Ujjayi (otherwise known as ocean breathing, where you start by breathing into the stomach and then the chest so that your body almost waves) when there is acute fear, each yoga position's relaxing effect is intensified so that the fear can be dissipated more quickly.

SOS for fear: breathing exercise in Adho Mukha Svanasana

To change the feeling of fear immediately, a specific form of inhalation and exhalation in the Adho-Mukha-Svanasana posture offers itself. This exercise is highly recommended when your anxiety threatens to escalate into uncontrollable panic. To be able to practice the breathing technique in the downward facing dog, start by assuming the position.

Method:

Remain relaxed in the downward-facing dog for five breaths. Now, with the next exhalation through your mouth, empty your lungs in spurts. Squeeze as much air out of your lungs as you can. Once you have emptied your lungs, close your mouth and maintain the vacuum in the lungs for as long as you comfortably can. When you can no longer refrain from inhaling, take a deep breath through your nose so that your lungs become maximally filled with air. Then breathe out again in bursts, entirely through your mouth and hold the vacuum in the lungs for a moment. Please repeat this breathing three times and then move into the child's pose to feel the effect.

If fear subsides, as the tension decreases, it often comes about that emotions dissolve. Admit it to yourself! When tears come, cry! Make sure that no destructive (overly intense) emotions are left unreleased. Crying is a healthy and normal response that releases tension and helps you regain balance.

Paschimottanasana - the forward bend

The Indians swear by the positive physical and psychological effects of this position. It is recommended because of its great benefits. It should give energy, strength and increase personal performance. This position also offers optimal help in many ways when it comes to alleviating the symptoms of anxiety. Not only does it help us to endure annoying physical and psychological reactions through the perception and acceptance of uncomfortable stretching pain, but it also teaches us to control our inner tension through breathing and thus to influence it positively.

The forward bend and its effect

The forward bend works in the abdomen by changing the flow of blood to the digestive tract. After the asana has been completed, more blood is transported to the abdominal area and has a detoxifying effect. Stubborn waste products and pollutants can be flushed out of the gastrointestinal tract. This gentle detoxification restores homeostasis in the intestine. A constant level of intestinal bacteria is in turn associated with a healthy psyche and a reduction in anxiety.

The positive influence of the forward bend by activating the vagus nerve also stimulates the immune system, activates the parasympathetic nervous system, and calms you down.

Warning: If you suffer from severely herniated discs, back injuries, or diarrhoea, this asana is not suitable for you. In such a case, please practice the other asana presented here and avoid the forward bend.

Method:

1.   Start in dandasana pose or more commonly known as the cane seat position. To do this, straighten your back, bring your shoulders back and pull them down a little so that your neck and neck area are relaxed. If possible, straighten your legs completely and bring your palms to the right and left of your hips. Now close your eyes for a moment and stay in this position.

2.   Now breathe in deeply through your nose and bring both arms to your sides and straight up above your head with your palms facing each other. Be careful not to tense your neck and keep your shoulders down. Your gaze follows the movement of your arms and thus also points upwards.

3.   With the next exhalation, slowly and consciously bring your upper body towards your thighs. If possible,

start with the lower abdomen, followed by the chest and finally the arms and head.

During this exercise, your gaze follows the movements of your arms.

Don't worry: most novice yoga practitioners find it impossible to get very far into the forward bend, especially at the beginning of the exercise. It is entirely acceptable only to bend as far as your limits allow and as far as you feel comfortable. The body quickly increases its movement amplitude, i.e. the expansion of the movement, to quickly adapt to the load and become more flexible. For as long as you can, try to remain in the pashimottanasana and slide your hands on your lower legs a centimetre more towards the tips of your feet with each further exhalation.

4.   When you have found the position that you can hold longer, stay down and, even with your head touching your legs, keep trying to bring your hands a little further forward and your head a little closer to your shins with each exhale. If you can touch your feet with your hands, grasp your big toes and pull your upper body towards your feet as you exhale.

When you have finished the paschimottanasana, feel and relax in the dandasana or in the Shavasana (laying down on your back). Stay as long as you need to relax completely. Try to stay entirely focused on yourself throughout the practice.

Be constantly aware of your breathing and observe the effects of the focused breathing on your body. You will find that exhaling allows you to increase the stretching of the muscles. Try not to cramp in the forward bend. This happens quickly in this position, as the stretching impulse in the back of the thigh is perceived as very uncomfortable or painful. Since we instinctively also want to avoid unpleasant physical sensations, the muscular opponent's contraction prevents further stretching during a short exercise period (less than five breaths).

The forward bend is a potent exercise. It strengthens the autonomic nervous system and teaches us acceptance

and patience with ourselves and our fear by confronting unpleasant physical sensations. The effect of Pashimottanasana on anxiety is very complex, as the parasympathetic nervous system can be activated in different ways. The positive impact of this position on the stomach and intestines, via the cleansing and peristalsis promoting effect of the intestine, leads to the internal milieu of the intestinal bacteria normalizing. It has long been known in science that "the stomach helps the head think" (Kast, 2009). So if we actively shape our gastrointestinal tract, it also influences our well-being and the expression of our fear.

Even within this exercise, the effect can be increased by holding longer. If we breathe Ujjayi, the calm will spread quickly in the body and pass over to the psyche.

Chapter 7

Fear of Change

Many people are afraid of change. The technical term is Metathesiophobia, sometimes also called neophobia, which is the fear of new things or change. We make ourselves comfortable in habits, routines and familiar things; when we encounter changes in this comfort zone we react with doubts, suspicion and fear.

You don't know precisely what is changing and what you are getting into. Leaving the security of the status quo is a fear of change. Why can't everything just stay the way it is? The problem: that's not how the world works. Not only is change a part of life but it is also a necessary part of it. This cannot be stopped - which is why you have to learn to deal with and overcome your fear of change. Don't make the mistake of closing yourself off for fear of change. I will show you where the fear of change comes from and what you can do to better cope with change.

Causes: where does fear of change come from?

It shouldn't come as a surprise to anyone that there have been all sorts of changes over the years. After school comes university or maybe an apprenticeship, very often in a new city, new apartment, new environment, new friends. It continues like this in both work and private life; time and again, there are turning points at which changes are inevitable. Nevertheless, many are caught unprepared, resist it and are afraid of these changes.

But why? There are several possible reasons and causes for fear of change:

Bad experiences

One possible cause is that you have had terrible experiences with change in the past. Anyone who has ever gone through a change that subsequently turned out to be a debacle does not want to experience something similar again. The past negative experience is often enough to stir up lasting fear of change. In the future, it will be assumed that every change to your circumstance will also go wrong.

Lack of self-confidence

A lack of self-confidence often causes the fear of change. You are afraid of not being able to adapt to the new situation. It is not changing itself that we fear. The fear of difference arises from the uncertainty of being able to deal with a change.

No control

Fear of change can also arise from a perceived loss of control. It is never possible to say in advance exactly what will change and whether this will go according to plan. The feeling of not being able to control these things leads to fear of change.

We have now looked at how change can make you feel but why does it make you feel that way?

Psychology of change

Upcoming changes allow a look into your psychology. How do you react? What is your approach to the matter? Are you afraid of the change, or are you optimistic? However, the circumstances must always be considered - changes can be divided into two types:

1. Voluntary changes

The first category is always the more pleasant. Every change here is self-initiated; it is performed out of choice and with a correspondingly high motivation level. In short: we want the difference, and we do our best for it.

Voluntary changes are changes you have chosen to make; for example, if the job is no longer fun, you hand in your resignation and reorient yourself, or if you voluntarily end your studies early to do an apprenticeship. Your impulse, decision, or change are a great advantage for the psychology behind it.

However even though the change was entered into voluntarily it does not mean that it will not garner fear but you will be better able to accept the changes and find it easier to overcome your anxiety because you have already decided to go through with it.

2. Involuntary changes

These are much more difficult. A fixed-term employment contract expires and will not be renewed even though you would like to stay with the company, your employer files for bankruptcy and you will inevitably have to change jobs or a relationship ends and you are forced into a position where you need to move house, there are all sorts of different examples of involuntary changes. Such unwanted steps can lead to a fear of change and initially to rejection of the change. It is difficult to see the chance; besides the fear of change, a forced change feels more like a burden. Such a change typically goes through five successive phases:

At first, the change is wholly refused, and its necessity is ignored. You pretend that everything can go on as normal. You may even offer resistance for fear of change. Everything is being done to stop the upcoming change.

With the realization that the resistance does not help, the peak of the crisis follows. Everything is questioned, and the fear of change is particularly significant.

From now on, things are looking up. New possibilities are explored and implemented step by step.

In the end, we realize that luckily it wasn't as bad as feared, and we accept the new situation. The fear of change is also diminishing or has already completely disappeared.

That is why you need to overcome the fear of change.

The key to success with changes is that it doesn't always have to be the huge step that changes everything at once and turns your previous life upside down. This is usually only necessary and inevitable when the time is right. Due to the fear of change, you have waited so long that it becomes all the more difficult. It is better to overcome the fear of change early on. Then even minor adjustments can have the desired impact. There are three good reasons to overcome the fear of change early rather than late:

1. You solve problems before they get worse.

Sure, in the beginning waiting is the easier way. You hope that things will work out by themselves and that problems will vanish as quickly as possible. Relying on it may work in some cases, but it is not generally a winning strategy. Usually, you have to do things yourself for something to improve.

If you act early, you have an advantage. Despite opposing hopes, problems have a nasty habit of tending to get bigger over time. In plain English: the later you start making the necessary changes, the more difficult it will be to fix the damage that has already occurred.

2. You keep your options open.

Not every door that has opened remains open. Most of your options are limited to a specific time frame - and once you have exceeded this, there is no turning back. Make yourself aware of this finality the next time you choose whether to leave everything at the status quo.

It also gives you the time it takes to make a wise and thoughtful decision about the change. You are not, yet, forced to act immediately; scrutinize the alternatives, and decide on the path that promises tremendous success.

3. You are continually improving.

An important, but unfortunately often underestimated, finding is that improvement is not a one-off event but a constant and ongoing process. It's not about making changes until the previous methods no longer work. Success is achieved by those who act proactively and consider possible changes even when there does not seem to be a need.

This can be observed again and again, especially in the corporate context. Successful companies don't wait for their business model to hit a dead end, for sales figures to drop, or for customers to switch to the competition. Instead, they are in an ongoing process of change and improvement.

How to deal with the fear of change

The question remains: what can you do to deal with your fear of change? It will not be easy because overcoming fears requires perseverance, discipline and a good deal of work. The following tips can help you face your fear of change and get it under control:

· **Stand by Your Fear**

There is no point in ignoring, belittling, or pretending your fear of change is not there. To overcome a fear, you have to face it.

The first step requires that you accept them and admit them to yourself.

· Talk About It

To better deal with the fear of change, it can help if you talk about it. Confide in your partner, a good friend, or even a psychiatrist. Explain what scares you and what you fear about upcoming changes. Such a conversation gives another perspective and helps against the fear of change because you get help and support.

· Make yourself aware of the worst case

Fear of change usually means fear of the worst case scenarios and consequences. What if everything goes wrong? Play this thought through to the end to see that even the worst-case scenario is often not that bad. Knowing what can happen in the worst-case gives you greater security.

· Look positively into the future

It is also essential to have the right mindset: Anyone who believes from the start that they will not cope with change only reinforces their fear. Instead, believe in yourself, encourage yourself, and recognize your strengths. Optimism is a perfect remedy for fear of change.

- · Take Small Steps

Fear of change is easier to master if you take small steps first. If possible, you don't have to change everything at once. It's easier to cope with minor adjustments and to get used to the new situation. In this way, you will also learn that there was no reason to be afraid of change and the next time you dare to do more.

Chapter 8

Deeper into the symptoms

What is agoraphobia?

The term agoraphobia is derived from Greek. The Greek word 'agora' means "marketplace" and 'phobia' is derived from the Greek word 'phobos' meaning "fear". This indicates that people with Agoraphobia are afraid of public places. However, those affected do not fear being cramped or enclosed in an internal space, instead they are scared of not escaping from there in an emergency or receiving no help. They also try to avoid situations where withdrawal due to an anxiety attack would be embarrassing - for example, during a theatre performance.

Unlike many other anxiety disorders, agoraphobia is not related to a specific situation or object. It can appear in very different places, such as in the cinema, on the bus or bridges. Without therapeutic help, agoraphobia leads to a severe reduction in the quality of life. Some no longer dare to go outside or need someone to accompany them and always have their medication and a cell phone with them in an emergency.

Agoraphobia and panic disorder

Agoraphobia occurs very often in combination with panic attacks. Around 35 to 56 percent of sufferers from panic or anxiety disorders have Agoraphobia with panic disorder. Panic attacks are violent anxiety attacks that usually last a few minutes. Those affected experience it as highly threatening because severe physical complaints also occur along with the psychological symptoms. These include rapid heart palpitations, sweating, dizziness, and many other symptoms that the sufferer perceives as life-threatening. This perception of being in a life-threatening situation causes the fear to increase more and more.

Fear of fear

A central characteristic of Agoraphobia is that those affected are afraid of possible panic or anxiety attacks in public. This phenomenon is known as 'fear of fear' or 'phobophobia'. The fear is also mostly reinforced since the fear of fear triggers physical tension. Those affected pay close attention to the minor material changes that could indicate a panic attack and are overly anxious. In the interplay of psyche and body, intense fear or even a panic attack can arise.

All the pondering and worrying in advance is at least as excruciating for them, if not worse, than the actual situation.

How many are affected?

Anxiety disorders are common. About four per cent of the population will suffer from Agoraphobia at least once in their life. Women are three times as likely to be affected as men. The onset of the mental disorder lies in late adolescence or young adulthood.

Very few people have pure Agoraphobia. Many also develop other anxiety disorders, but also depression, alcohol addictions and personality disorders.

Agoraphobia: symptoms

For the diagnosis of Agoraphobia, those affected must show specific symptoms according to the ICD-10 (International Classification of Diseases revision 10) classification of mental disorders.

As the main criterion, sufferers must avoid or strongly and persistently fear at least two of the following situations:

Crowds

Public places

Travel alone

Travelling far from home

Also, at least two of the following physical or psychological anxiety symptoms must be present, which also occur together.

Physical symptoms

People with Agoraphobia always have one or more of the following symptoms:

Palpitations (increased heart rate)

Sweating

Trembling

Dry mouth

Difficulty breathing

Anxiety

Chest pain or discomfort

Nausea or feeling unwell in your stomach

Feeling dizzy, unsteady, weak, or light-headed

Psychological symptoms

Feeling that oneself or the environment are not real
(depersonalization or derealization)

Fear of losing control

Fear of going crazy

Fear of dying

Common mental symptoms

Most people with Agoraphobia fear panic attacks or
fainting attacks in public. All patients with Agoraphobia fear
crowds. However, the reasons for this are different. People
who have pure Agoraphobia without panic attacks are
more likely to fear embarrassing situations, such as being
afraid to wet themselves. In Agoraphobia with panic
attacks, it is less the embarrassment of the anxiety attacks
that trouble the sufferer than the fear of not receiving help
and dying due to the physical symptoms.

Those affected suffer a lot from their fears. However, you
know that these are excessive. This knowledge alone does
not, however, tame anxiety. It gets stronger over time and
occurs when you only imagine the dreaded situation. I use

the word 'tame' rather than fight as to fight anxiety you are only fighting yourself and will never win but to tame it you are learning how to control it and focus less on the physical symptoms.

At first, they only avoid a few places; later on, hardly anywhere seems safe. They severely limit their leisure activities, and doing their work also becomes a challenge. Agoraphobia, therefore, has profound effects, both professionally and financially, as well as in private and social life. This is how it affected me.

Agoraphobia: causes and risk factors

Hereditary component

There can be a hereditary component of Agoraphobia. Children whose parents have Agoraphobia are at increased risk of developing this mental disorder as well. The messenger substances in the brain also influence development. Malfunctions of the serotonin and noradrenaline-releasing systems are possible causes. Whether the disease develops, however, also largely depends on psychosocial factors.

Stress as a cause

Stressful activities increase the likelihood of Agoraphobia in people who are prone to fear. People with Agoraphobia often had traumatic experiences in childhood. Sometimes, the loss of a parent through death or divorce, personal illness or sexual abuse can later contribute to an anxiety disorder. Stress can also trigger agoraphobia in adulthood. Also people in healthy relationships are less likely to suffer from an anxiety disorder than single people due to having a built in support structure and the removal of the sense of isolation.

Fear sensitivity

Some people are more sensitive to vast amounts of sensory information around them, the constant barrage of social and media data through phones, the internet or TV is not something that our brains have learned to process yet and therefore people with a lower tolerance to this information are more prone to agoraphobia. They perceive physical changes, such as palpitations more firmly and perceive them as threatening. Often they then imagine catastrophic scenarios. The result is fear, which in turn increases the physical symptoms.

In many cases, agoraphobia begins with a panic attack. In a public space that to the casual observer would be considered safe, those affected suddenly experience strong body reactions such as a racing heart or dizziness. Such complaints can initially be caused or exacerbated by the consumption of coffee, low blood sugar or other physiological factors.

The panic attacks actual trigger is that those affected overestimate the symptoms and experience them as a threat.

Psychological factors

A major factor contributing to anxiety is the feeling of not having control over the physical reactions during the state of anxiety. Therefore, those affected avoid unknown places. They fear that they are helplessly at the mercy of the situation and the strangers around them.

Agoraphobia: examinations and diagnosis

At the start of treatment, a doctor will perform a medical examination to rule out physical illnesses as the cause. Several physical problems can trigger severe anxiety. These include some diseases like heart problems, thyroid and lung diseases or disorders of balance. The examination consists of a blood count and an electrocardiogram (EKG/ECG) to check the heart. If necessary, the doctor will carry out further investigations.

To determine if your fears are psychological, the doctor may ask you the following questions:

'Do you ever experience severe anxiety related to physical symptoms, such as palpitations, sweating, or shortness of breath?'

'Have you avoided an event for fear of an anxiety attack?'

'When you are in a public place, how do you feel?'

If your responses to the doctor's questions correlate with agoraphobia disorder, the doctor will most likely refer you to an outpatient psychotherapist or a psychosomatic clinic. A psychotherapist or psychologist can make a more accurate diagnosis. Using a questionnaire, the specialist can determine whether any other mental disorders are present that require treatment.

Agoraphobia: treatment

Psychotherapy and medication are used for agoraphobia therapy. Experts particularly recommend cognitive behavioural therapy for the treatment of agoraphobia. Psychodynamic psychotherapy is an alternative, this is a form of therapy that delves into the subconscious in an effort to alleviate anxiety.

Anecdotally there are a number of herbal options that some claim can help alleviate symptoms, the most popular of these options at the moment is CBD oil which can be inhaled, eaten or applied topically. Sufferers that have tried CBD oil for a prolonged period have claimed to see a reduction in their symptoms. For example a reduction in night terrors or a better quality of sleep.

Cognitive-behavioural therapy (CBT)

Cognitive-behavioural therapy starts with excessive fearful thoughts and works on removing avoidance/coping strategies that you have developed over time. For successful treatment, you have to deal intensively with their fears.

Nowadays therapists refer to the confrontation with scary places and situations as exposure. Patients are encouraged to expose themselves to situations where symptoms of anxiety or panic occur. After exposure, you report what symptoms they experienced during the exercise. As part of the therapy, you experience first-hand that, for example, the faster heartbeat is not life-threatening and goes back down on its own after a while. You experience that the fear of fear is worse than the experience itself. A major component to CBT is that the body can only maintain a state of panic or anxiety for a limited amount of time so eventually even if you stay in that situation the panic or anxiety will lessen. Four pieces of information need to be recorded during the exposure exercise, firstly the anxiety level (as a percentage) before the exposure, second the anxiety level (as a percentage) at the start of the exposure, thirdly the anxiety level (as a percentage) at the end of the exposure and lastly the duration of the exercise. An example of a CBT diary is below:

Date	Duration	What are you doing	Before	Start	End	Comments
14/04	00:31:19	Shops	50%	60%	35%	Quieter than expected but still terrifying.
15/04	00:23:31	Shops	55%	65%	30%	Hit me harder than yesterday but seemed to reduce quicker

| 16/04 | 00:27:35 | Shops | 60% | 70% | 20 % | Busier time,very uncomfortable at the start but anxiety rapidly reduced |
| 19/04 | 00:22:54 | Shops | 20% | 30% | 15 % | anxiety levels were relatively low going in, spiked a few time |

The therapist also teaches you to observe thoughts closely and to recognize unrealistic fears. The severity of the mental disorder is not related to the intensity or frequency of the anxiety symptoms but to how dangerous you perceive them. Therefore, the review and, if necessary, the revision of thoughts and the appropriate interpretation of physical reactions are essential to the therapy. They enable the decisive steps to be able to overcome the fear of fear.

Over time, there will be fewer and fewer places where the fear occurs. After about fifteen sessions, most patients can enter many dreaded situations without fear.

Psychodynamic psychotherapy

In the context of psychodynamic psychotherapy, the therapist assumes that there is an unresolved conflict behind the anxiety symptoms. This conflict must be recognized and dealt with so that the fear can be overcome. For example, it can be about separation, suppressed anger or even sexual problems. The therapist's concern is to make unconscious processes clear in the conversation so that you can recognize and process them.

Additional treatment measures

In addition to therapy, experts also recommend physical activity. Endurance training or heightened physical activity is said to help improve symptoms.

Participation in self-help groups is also often helpful for those affected and can reinforce the fact that you are not alone.

A healthy sex life (if appropriate) can also help to alleviate psychological issues.

Agoraphobia: disease course and prognosis

Agoraphobia often starts suddenly with the first attack of anxiety in a public place. Only in a few cases does the mental disorder go away on its own. Without treatment, agoraphobia is usually chronic. The longer the mental illness persists, the more likely it is for other related issues to develop, such as alcohol abuse or depressive symptoms.

Agoraphobia often runs in phases. The condition of those affected can fluctuate from day to day. The symptoms of anxiety can reappear even after a long period of symptom-free treatment.

The earlier patients seek therapeutic help, the better the prognosis usually is. In particular, exposure therapy has helped many people cope with their agoraphobia and regain their lives.

How can panic and staying at home lead to agoraphobia?

The global response to the coronavirus pandemic made simply not leaving your home somewhat different to having agoraphobia. The pandemic can, however, increase agoraphobic tendencies due to the enforced isolation.

Millions of people were quarantined due to the corona pandemic, there were 11 million in Wuhan (China) alone. This is not without consequences for the population, the affected people, relatives and especially the medical staff: They have to deal with extreme emotions of panic, shock, confusion, anger, grief, guilt and helplessness. This acute crisis led to many psychosomatic and psychological complaints. These must also be taken into account in crisis management.

Months of pandemic shelter and non-stop news coverage on the dangers of COVID-19 contracted by others, or high-touch surfaces provided a perfect storm for agoraphobia. The pandemic and quarantine could have pushed people over the edge who were still at increased risk for the condition. Between January 2020 and May 2021 global cases of panic and anxiety grew three fold as a direct result of lockdowns leading to isolation and separation, this was a conservative estimation made by a handful of European universities. That being said as a result of the

COVID-19 pandemic awareness of mental health issues increased dramatically.

Increasing agoraphobia risk factors include:

Having another fear, like panic, widespread anxiety or obsessive compulsive disorder.

Having other phobias, such as hypochondria (excessive and undue fear of having a serious illness), mysophobia/germophobia (fear of dirt and germs) or nosocomephobia (fear of hospitals)

Traumatic experience

Traumatic Brain Injury (TBIs)

How Quarantine Impacts People who have Agoraphobia already

Pandemic and stay at home orders may have caused increased seriousness of the symptoms in people already affected by agoraphobia. Those who have managed their condition previously may have suffered more in the pandemic situation.

Listening to the news about breathing difficulties can remind them of panic symptoms that can cause anxiety. The concept of self isolation can give rise to fears of being trapped or fear of exposure to others, especially if you have an underlying physical health condition.

Physical Brain Activity and Agoraphobia

Functional brain imaging tests suggest that agoraphobia and other phobias may not be simply mental health issues but rather a physical issue within the brain. They could be a symptom of that physical issue. Available studies in brain imaging using SPECT technologies show that people with a phobia, such as agoraphobia, tend to have an overactivity in an area of the brain known as the Basal Ganglia.

One woman stayed home for 40 years before finally leaving to have a brain scan. By seeing her brain's abnormal function, she realised that her phobias were not her fault and that there was a physical cause for her issues helped her to come to terms with her condition.

Managing Agoraphobia

Agoraphobia can be managed at home. Healthy lifestyle habits include the following:

- Eliminate caffeine, nicotine and alcohol consumption
- Regularly engage in physical activity, but avoid exercise of high intensity that can cause fear
- Sleep every night for at least 7 hours
- Eat foods that are nutritious and avoid sweets
- Meditate or pray to soothe the fearful brain
- Stay in contact even if you cannot meet in person with friends and family
- Consider brain-improving supplements, such as various complex vitamin-minerals, fatty acids omega-3 and vitamin D

If you leave home and start to panic – whether it's in the shop, in a park or the mall. Slow your breathing. You'll increase your blood oxygen by taking long, deep breaths and begin to regain control over how you feel.

Write down your thoughts. Write down your feelings. These should be reviewed at least weekly and then any that you identify as being warped thoughts or feelings should be looked at more deeply so you can work out better ways to view the situation.

Searching for help

You should seek treatment if you feel like you are getting close to a breaking point or being pushed over the edge and developing agoraphobia. The sooner you get help, the more beneficial it will be. If your symptoms worsen, do not hesitate to seek the care of a therapist or doctor.

Dealing with agoraphobia, other phobias and anxieties cannot wait. Your mental well-being is more critical than ever in these uncertain times, you may find that after seeking help your symptoms may intensify or become worse before life returns to "normal".

Chapter 9

Stress

Definition of stress

You are already running late anyway, then the bus leaves just as you get to the door, and at work, countless emails with urgent to do's are waiting for you while your colleague is urgently waiting for your feedback. Probably every one of us knows stressful situations in everyday life, and now and then wishes just to be able to press the 'pause' button.

But how do you define stress? The term stress originally comes from the field of mechanics and describes an external force that leads to deformation or pressure. The Hungarian-Canadian physician and biochemist Hans Selye first introduced the term stress into medicine and is therefore considered the father of stress research. He gave a fairly general definition that describes stress as "the body's non-specific response to a request".

Stress is not harmful. There are situations in which it is pretty helpful and moves us forward - yes, it can even drive our body to peak performance. Because those outside effects are cause triggering stress (the so-called stressors) put our body in a necessary alarm state, which mobilizes our energy reserves and, from an evolutionary perspective, makes us ready for the attack or flight. The stress hormones cortisol, insulin, adrenaline and noradrenaline are released within a short time, the positive impact when these hormones are released the senses become sharp and the focus is increased and the muscles are tensed.

Need of stress

How you react to these stressors is usually subjective. If for instance you are a passionate surfer, the wind and waves give you the adrenaline rush you need to ride the waves providing you with increased endurance and subsequently enjoyment. If you love the beach as a sun lover, you may find the idea of getting into the sea as threatening or frightening, and you don't dare to cool off in the water. It is precisely the same on an aeroplane: while one person may be enjoying the flight and can doze off relaxed, another spends the entire flight with palpitations and beads of sweat on their forehead and cannot wait to land.

There are also stressors that almost everyone perceives as stressful, some common examples of these are heat, noise, crowds, bullying or contact with people who are not suitable for you.

As is so often the case with stress, the following applies: The dose makes the poison. The longer, more frequent and more intense pressure is, the unhealthier it is. Each person also has unique limits on how much pressure they can endure. A phase of recovery must follow every single tension.

Unfortunately, the tension (anxiety or other continous stressors) and the stress hormones released are no longer wholly reduced by a resting state. Therefore, your body is in a permanent state of alarm, which requires energy and leads to a state of exhaustion in the long term. Concentration disorders, fatigue and digestive disorders can occur as a result. In the worst case, stress can also lead to burnout. For this reason, sufficient recovery periods are all the more critical. Did you copy and paste this section?

How do we experience stress, and what causes it?

Stress is relative. When, where and how we experience it is entirely subjective. Everyone experiences it in different ways, and everyone reacts differently. What stresses one person can leave another wholly relaxed.

What is the same, however, are the processes in our body. Adrenaline and noradrenaline are released, and the body is put on alert. The result? Our body is under tension to be able to cope better with psychological and physical challenges. Some bodily functions are increased, others shut down.

Some people relax pretty quickly, others take hours to come back down and turn off the carousel of thought. For some, distraction helps; for others, relaxation or letting go of the topic.

Stress is also a matter of attitude and has a lot to do with our attitude towards situations. It arises through the emotional processing of problems - how we assess the situation determines our reaction to it.

Recognizing stressors: what are the most common stressors?

According to stress researcher Dr Hans Selye, stress is the "unspecific reaction of the organism to any kind of stressor". Stressors are the stimuli that cause stress. A distinction is made

between:

• physical stressors (external or internal stimuli that put a strain on the body)

• psychological stressors (psychological reaction to influencing factors)

• social stressors (partnerships, family, the social environment)

• biochemical stressors (drugs, alcohol, chemicals)

Do you keep a stress log?

Keeping a stress log or a stress diary could help you to cope better with existing stressful situations and at the same time make it easier for you to deal with future stresses.

The aim is to identify factors that trigger stress through self-observation and work on them in a targeted manner. First, over one week, record all events and things that cause stress in you. Write everything down, regardless of whether it's the morning rush hour, deadline pressure, anger at colleagues or a friend ignoring you / cancelling on you.

You can also create a table for this. It is essential to assign the feeling of stress to the actual trigger. Also, rate your stress level with each of your entries. For example, slightly stressed - tolerable - heavily stressed. Or through the evaluation with numbers from 1 (slightly stressed) to 5 (very heavily stressed).

You can also expand your table by noting how the stressful situation came about and how exactly you reacted to it. Have a look to see whether there is a specific pattern behind your way of responding. Also make sure to note down to what extent your feeling of stress was justified. Sometimes the objective observation of one's behaviour alone can make one aware of a lot.

STRESS MANAGEMENT METHODS

What stresses us and how it affects us and our health is very individual. Stress in moderation is beneficial and can help us to top shape, both physically and mentally. However, if the stress lasts for too long, it can be damaging to our health. Regular relaxation phases, in which your stress levels subside and you relax, are critical.

You have to find out for yourself what this relaxation looks like for you. You must do something good for yourself and that changes your mind. With the tips and tricks in this chapter, I have given you a few suggestions on how you can counteract stress in a targeted manner. You don't always need a lot of time for this, because even short breaks can have many positive effects. And even if there are only minor changes that you make, they help you deal with stress healthily and go through your everyday life in a more balanced way, because this is the only way you can draw new energy!

Most people certainly know the feeling of not doing what you would like to do and instead feeling rushed to try to complete these tasks that you would rather not be doing.

It's uncomfortable and has a massive impact on our well-being. The earlier you recognize the problem of stress and tackle it, the faster your well-being increases and the faster you can do something for your health.

Everyone has to find their own way to deal with stress, and the possibilities are diverse:

- Consciously allow yourself a moment of rest

- Get enough sleep

- Use relaxation techniques to build stress

- Promote stress relief through proper nutrition

- Reduce stress through exercise

- Think positively

- Do some yoga!

Regardless of what you choose, the most important thing is - main thing is that you are fully involved and consciously take the time to do something for yourself and your health.

Consciously allow yourself a moment to rest.

Small breaks in between help you to concentrate better afterwards. Even the slightest break can have a significant impact.

Lean back in your office chair and consciously allow yourself a few minutes of distraction or a few minutes to do something else. This can often work wonders because it is essential to break the constant tension.

Go out into nature and take in all impressions consciously because the character has a calming effect on most people. For example, read a book, have a quiet cup of tea or enjoy the sun for a few minutes on a park bench during your lunch break.

Everyone finds different strategies to deal with stress and protect themselves from its consequences. While some can relax with a good book, it helps others to exercise or to garden. In a 2018 Statista survey on counter stress measures, "Relaxing and lazing around" and "Watching TV" came first with 49 per cent each. Listening to music, going for a walk, gardening and meeting family and friends were also found to be popular ways of combating stress.

I have put together six other tips for you to let go of stress and relax. These small, regular breaks are suitable for your body and mind and help you recharge your batteries and go through everyday life in a more relaxed manner.

Tip 1: relaxation

Relaxation is an essential tool in dealing with stress. Various relaxation techniques can help you deal better with stressful situations. Used regularly, they can significantly increase wellbeing and provide more balance.

Important - it is about active relaxation with the help of various relaxation techniques and not about passive relaxation. For example, you lie down on the sofa in the evening and let the television wash over you.

Relaxation begins first and foremost in mind. It works best when you manage to interrupt the constant stream of thoughts in your head so that you can calm down.

The term 'relaxation' already says it all. The goal is to relieve tension and get into a state in which body, mind, and soul balance. Pressure, anxiety and stress fall away from you as you relax. In today's society, in particular, relaxation methods such as autogenic training (a desensitization relaxation technique) and meditation are becoming increasingly popular. The focus here is entirely on yourself and conscious breathing, thus letting go of tension. If you haven't tried it yet, you should give it a go! And don't worry, meditation courses or similar don't always have to lapse into esotericism. There are so many choices of courses available now that there is sure to be one that is right for you Reduce stress and relax through yoga. As we covered earlier in this book yoga should help you to find inner peace and relaxation. With various physical and breathing exercises, the tension of stressful everyday life should be relieved. The effects are diverse and range from an improvement in concentration to more energy and vitality to increase physical fitness and self-confidence.

Studies have already shown the positive effect of yoga on the perception of stress. Relaxing hatha yoga, in particular, is a popular method for reducing stress. If you need a little more action, you can try the more dynamic Ashtanga Yoga.

However, if you find that the relaxation techniques mentioned above are not for you, there are, of course, other short-term and quickly applicable measures that will help you to calm down and destress. For example, hold your wrists under cold water for a short moment or take a deep breath and then try to breathe consciously for two or three breaths. You can also count back from 20 to zero or force yourself to smile for at least 60 seconds. Even if that sounds absurd at first, studies show that a fake smile or laugh also helps to release happiness hormones (the so-called endorphins) so that you feel much more relaxed afterwards, we will look more into breather exercises later in this chapter.

Tip 2: Get enough sleep

Deep, restful sleep is the best medicine for too much stress. Unfortunately, this is often easier said than done because you sleep worse when under increased pressure. You quickly take the problems with you to bed and deprive yourself of healthy sleep.

Doing relaxation before going to sleep can help calm your mind and spirit to fall asleep more quickly. Small rituals before going to bed often help to develop a routine and to be able to switch off better.

There are many recommendations for optimal sleep length; most studies recommend between seven and eight hours. But here, too, you have to find out your individual sleep needs for yourself. Listen to your body and its signals because you understand it best. If your eyes repeatedly close during the day, or you are exhausted and can only keep yourself awake with caffeinated drinks; you should adjust your sleep quota.

Ensure that you only sleep in your bed and don't get distracted by other things like social media. Shifting your bedtime and getting up times can also help you feel more awake in the morning and to feel more energetic throughout the day.

Incidentally, it has been proven that it can be more difficult to fall asleep if you look at your smartphone shortly before going to bed. The blue light on the display means that your body produces less of the sleep hormone melatonin and that you don't feel tired as a result. So it's best to put your cell phone away at least half an hour before going to bed. If due to work or other commitments, you need to use your phone or computer before bed there are a variety of applications available that will slowly reduce the blue light emitted by the device during the evening in order to help maintain a healthy circadian rhythm.

Tip 3: get enough exercise

By the way, we don't just reduce stress when we relax. We can also lower our stress level while moving. And a little encouragement for those who don't like sports: exercise is most useful when you don't overdo it. Whether strength training in the gym, relaxation methods such as QiGong, yoga or a simple walk in the great outdoors - there are many ways to reduce your cortisol(one of the stress hormones) level . In any case, you must choose an activity that you enjoy and that suits you. Because if you force yourself to do an activity just because it is currently in fashion or because others have persuaded you to do it, stress may be triggered again.

And if you are feeling a bit more active then traditional sport is a proven method to compensate for a stressful everyday life. Exercise and physical activity help reduce stress in the body. The stress hormones are lowered back to normal levels. That is why endurance sports are particularly suitable. For example

- To run

- Nordic walking

- Inline skating

- Bicycle riding

Exercise can serve as a valve for the pressure built up in our body due to stressful situations.

Tip 4: time management

Even if you may not like to hear it, good time management can save you from a lot of stress. Because if you plan enough time for all the to-do's during the day and also have a bit of buffer for unexpected events, then stress often can be prevented for arising in the first place. Structured daily or weekly planning provides you with the necessary framework conditions to have enough time to act. You can react in a more relaxed way even in the event of unforeseeable, urgent circumstances. Also, you have a good overview of what to expect during the week and can prepare yourself mentally for it.

Tip 5: a balanced diet

Under stress, your brain only knows one goal: energy! And it gets that by forcing you to take in as many calories as possible. Calories are found in carbohydrates, fats, and sugar. And who has not encountered that infamous chocolate bar that gets grabbed when the stress gets out of hand again? Unfortunately, we often resort to sweets and fast food in stressful situations - after all, it has to be quick. But even if the chocolate initially helps, unhealthy foods make your symptoms of stress worse. The sugar will give you a short push, but then your blood sugar will drop rapidly, and you will fall into a deep energy hole.

Or maybe you are someone whose stomach literally constricts under stress and who eats almost nothing? In both cases, a balanced, high-energy and healthy diet is essential. You can find them in fresh and raw foods. These contain the vitamins and minerals that are important for your body. And ultimately ensure that a body can deal better with stress. As for that overwhelming desire for sweet food that can come from stress rather than going for the chocolate bar a slice of wholemeal toast with natural honey can satiate the desire for sweets whilst also not being as harsh on the body as processed sugars.

A balanced diet is indispensable, especially since it is often neglected in today's stressful everyday life. Most of the time, you just devour something in between meals, and often you grab something unhealthy from the bakery next door or the nearest fast-food restaurant.

However, only a body that is adequately supplied can cope with increased stress levels accordingly. In the long run, inadequate, unhealthy nutrition makes us dissatisfied, irritable and more sensitive to stress more quickly.

When shopping, make sure you buy healthy, fresh and balanced foods and take your time to prepare them. Another good option is to cook a little more so you can take another serving with you for lunch the next day. If you don't like to eat the same thing twice in a row, you can, of course, prepare something separately for the lunch break the next day. In this way, due to the lack of time, one simply avoids taking "anything" for a short time.

And very important: take your time for the food itself. If we eat too quickly and gobble everything down hastily, it only puts additional strain on our digestion. This is already suffering from stress, so why harm our well-being even more? Chew slowly and thoroughly, consciously enjoying your meals.

Tip 6: conflict management

We all know it; conflicts stress us out. Regardless of whether they are of a private or professional nature. Of course, it cannot be avoided entirely when people with different views and values meet. The magic words here are 'conflict management'. If you master this skill, you will find it much easier to deal with conflicts, and you will feel less stressed by differences of opinion.

Deeper Dive into Stress management

Now that we have covered an overview of stress management and my six top tips we are going to take a deeper look at some of the other things you can do to manage your stress levels.

Reduce stress through meditation

Meditation has been a relaxation method that has been practised for centuries, especially in Asia. It should ensure a clear mind and help to get out of the vortex of thoughts. Mindful breathing and conscious arrival in the body. Allow yourself some rest, don't have to do anything and, above all, don't think anything.

One concentrates on certain parts of the body, breathing, a positive feeling, a mantra or specific images to calm the mind.

Meditation does, however, require a bit of practice. People who are constantly electrified can initially have difficulties sitting or lying down and focusing on their breathing.

Various breathing exercises can be an excellent introduction to this.

Reduce stress through breathing exercises

The role of breathing is often underestimated, and it is essential. Because when we are under stress, our breathing is significantly accelerated. In the state of relaxation, however, calmly and evenly. Therefore, conscious breathing can help calm down in moments of tension.

A few short breathing exercises can be quickly put in between, even in a stressful everyday life. They are practical and effective, especially in acutely stressful situations when you are about to lose your nerve. They can be done anytime, anywhere, including in the office, and they only take a few minutes.

Count breaths

Sit upright in a chair and relax your shoulders and neck area.

Now breathe in and out only through your nose. Breathe evenly and calmly into your stomach. Then pause for 2 seconds between inhaling and exhaling - without suddenly holding your breath.

In the next step, count to five each as you inhale and exhale. As you can handle this, increase the inhalation and exhalation times by gradually counting to ten.

Concentrate only on your breaths and the air flowing in and out. Also, you can consciously let anything negative flow out of your body when you breathe out.

Concentrating on breathing helps to direct the focus away from the problems and bring clarity to the head.

Stress reduction through "MBSR".

MBSR means "Mindfulness-based Stress Reduction", which means something like "Mindfulness-based stress reduction". It is an approach to stress management based on the principle of mindfulness. This technique was initially developed by the US medical professor Jon Kabat-Zinn and consisted of a combination of:

- Mindful body awareness

- meditation

- yoga

It has been proven to lead to a relevant reduction in stress. In this way, the levels of stress, depression and anxiety in elementary school teachers who had attended an MBSR course were significantly reduced.

Reduce stress through autogenic training

With the help of autogenic training, a comprehensive deep relaxation of body and mind can be achieved. Suggestive formulas such as "My right leg is heavy" draws attention to different parts of the body one after the other, which can bring about a state of relaxation.

The head is focused on the body's corresponding areas and is thus distracted by constantly recurring thought patterns. Stress relief through progressive muscle relaxation

Jacobson's advanced muscle relaxation technique reduces the muscular tension in the body when we are energized in everyday life. The principle is relaxation through tensing.

Certain areas of the body are first consciously tensed and then relaxed one after the other. Usually, the tension is held between 5 and 10 seconds. In between, you feel the state of relaxation in your body.

This should gradually achieve a relaxed state in the entire body.

Reduce stress through dream trips

Use your imagination and start a short fantasy journey to break the stressful everyday life. Go in your mind to a place you like, for example, your last vacation spot or a beautiful forest clearing. Try to imagine everything that evokes a positive feeling (scents, colours, experiences) in as much detail as possible.

Let the excellent feeling flow through your whole body and enjoy it to the full. Then it is easier to dedicate your thoughts to the tasks at hand.

The power of thoughts: think positively

Sometimes there is simply nothing we can do to change stressful circumstances—appointments that merely cannot be postponed or exams that you just have to take. What we can change, however, is our attitude towards it. Because illusion simply doesn't make things any better. Sentences like "I can never do that!" Are not exactly beneficial.

Our thoughts can both strengthen and weaken us. So, for a change, use your thoughts to enhance yourself by motivating yourself with positive sentences. The key is to counter negative thoughts with positive ones.

Become aware of the extent of your stress. You can also formulate your thoughts in writing and organize them as an aid. The precise formulation of your thoughts and worries on paper ensures awareness and helps to get to the root of the problem because constant brooding doesn't get further.

For a change, try to see difficulties not as threats but as challenges.

Often it also helps to think of something that you are looking forward to or a pleasant experience from the past. The positive feeling that this creates in one lifts the mood and helps to lower the stress level.

Coping with stress is not only a question of technique but also a question of one's attitude. Check your attitudes and ways of thinking: Do we always have to make life so difficult for ourselves? Do we always have to be perfect, stay strong and just not show any weakness?

Be aware of the good and the positive to feel gratitude.

Dealing with stress properly: learning to cope with stress

Stress management is the use of specific strategies to reduce or relieve feelings of anxiety. Often referred to as stress management. They help to maintain health and performance and to strengthen individual skills in coping with stress.

Successful stress management starts on the one hand with the individual handling of stress-inducing factors and on the other hand with the body's reactions to stress.

Typical areas of focus in improving stress management tend to be:

• conveying information on how to deal with stress

• identify individual stressors and develop coping strategies

• Use stress-energy positively

• learning short-term relief techniques

• learning long-term stress reduction and coping techniques

The strategies for coping with stress in everyday life, how they can be learned and best integrated into everyday life are explained in more detail below.

If you find it more difficult to work alone to improve your stress management, you can get help in the form of consultations, coaching, seminars and group courses.

What strategies for coping with stress can I learn?

You can learn to cope with stress actively. The possibilities for this are diverse and can be easily integrated into everyday life. Often, a change in attitude to stress can effectively influence the body's response to stress.

Relevant evaluation studies have already proven the effectiveness of stress management training to reduce physical complaints and psychological effects (depression, anxiety).

Tip 1: Learn to say "No!"

Saying "no" is one of the most challenging things for a lot of people. It is important to set oneself apart and reject other people from time to time, not constantly to pass something on to them. Of course, that does not mean that from now on, we will no longer be helpful.

However, those who cannot say "no" will only become more frustrated and dissatisfied with themselves in the long run.

Tip 2: what is my time management like?

Good organization is half the battle. Proper time management can save you from a lot of frustration and additional stress. Because many stressful situations only arise from the inadequate organization. Those who are well organized and keep an eye on their appointments can lower their stress level a lot.

Think about it beforehand: What can I achieve at what time? What is realistic? You might want to allow a little more time not to put yourself under too much pressure.

In this way, you avoid constantly having a bad feeling or a guilty conscience because you have supposedly failed to do something again.

Tip 3: write a to-do list

A good option is to create to-do lists to get an overview of all the tasks to be completed and to be able to assess how much time which job takes.

It is better to set yourself a lot of smaller goals instead of a few big goals. This creates a sense of achievement, and the upcoming tasks do not seem so huge that you are more confident to tackle them.

Work through one point at a time and try to avoid wanting to do everything simultaneously.

And the best thing about to-do lists is that they can feel perfect for crossing out one more item than done. Also, it is very motivating to see what you have already achieved.

Tip 4: Am I setting my priorities correctly?

It makes sense to set priorities for all tasks. Both in work life and in private. What is essential and needs to be done immediately? What can just as quickly be done at a later point in time?

Sort all upcoming tasks according to their priority. This helps to work in a more structured and consistent manner and not lose sight of the essentials.

Stress is often a question of your standards. Intense perfectionism can be a hindrance, especially in stressful situations.

Tip 5: Set limits for yourself

Communicate your needs clearly and distinctly, and don't be afraid to set boundaries consciously. This is important for you and others because you can't expect other people to notice when they might be asking too much automatically.

Therefore, it is essential to make your limits clear and ensure that they are adhered to.

Tip 6: Make precise arrangements

Make precise arrangements to avoid stress with those around you. Clarify things in advance and create framework conditions that you can easily adhere to. Communicate your needs clearly and precisely.

Tip 7: Accept the stressful state

This may sound a bit strange to one or the other at first, but one of the most fundamental points in coping with stress is to recognize the condition as such. At a certain point, there is simply no point in telling yourself that you can do more.

That only helps one thing: being honest with yourself. There is no shame in admitting that you are overwhelmed.

Tip 8: Take advantage of moments of relaxation

Consciously doing nothing - some people have to learn that first because we are used to using every second and working effectively. Treat yourself to your quiet times when you are not approachable or available to anyone. Make a conscious decision to switch off all communication media (cell phone, PC, social networks).

Tip 9: Listen to your gut instinct

You should always listen to your gut instinct. What doesn't feel good should be reconsidered. It doesn't help to take on every project and every task when the alarm bells are already ringing inside, because you know very well that everything is too much for you.

Tip 10: stay mindful

Focus on the here and now, no matter what you're doing. Stay attentive and try to consciously go through the little things of everyday life, whether you climb a few stairs or just wash your hands for a moment.

Experience things very consciously without thinking about a hundred other things. Anyone who is already thinking about what else has to be done while doing what they are doing comes under pressure.

Besides, it can be constructive to directly stop stress-inducing thoughts such as "I have to do this today". Whenever you catch yourself with such a thought, you can sit back, take a few deep breaths in and out and calm yourself down to reduce the stress level a little.

Tip 11: Learn to act independently

Most of all, stress arises when we get the impression that we have no control over things that happen to us, but at the same time, we are asked to be able to deal with them. That is why it is essential to act in a self-determined manner instead of being determined by others. The tips mentioned so far can help you with this.

Tip 12: Address problems

Communicate your problems openly, both professionally and privately. Talk to colleagues or supervisors about the feasibility of goals that sound unattainable.

Communicate openly and honestly with your partner or family members. This can prevent false expectations and save unnecessary trouble.

Tip 13: Don't take your work home with you

That, too, is easier said than done. Many people take their work home with them because they just can't switch off. This makes it harder to recover and give the body time to regenerate.

Perhaps it helps to simply switch off the business cell phone after leaving the office and no longer constantly check company emails after work.

Tip 14: A stable social environment has a supportive effect

Social contacts are important to us humans. So spend your time with people who like you and who are good for you. It helps to have a trusted person to open up to and share with. Sometimes it is enough to just talk about it all.

Can you learn how to cope with stress incorrectly?

Several different behaviour patterns suggest that coping with stress was learned incorrectly. Those affected follow specific patterns and behaviours that they have become accustomed to over many years because coping with stress was unknown.

Often this is expressed in certain behaviours towards other people. A distinction is made between aggressive, evasive and resigned behaviour patterns.

For example, aggressive can be:

- Taking medication to improve performance

- Striving for perfection

- Bullying other people as compensation

- radical rejection of tasks

Evasive behaviour can be shown by:

- frequent breaks

- Daydreams

- Increased consumption or addiction behaviour

- Change of job

Resigned behaviour can sometimes be:

- total ignoring or repressing problems

- Constant brooding

- advocate own helplessness

- inaction

Stress prevention tips: What methods can I use to prevent stress?

Anyone who tries to deal more optimistically and confidently with demanding situations can reduce stress from the outset.

According to the transactional stress model of psychologist Richard Lazarus, the emergence of stress can be traced back to the interaction between requirements and the individual assessment of one's resources and abilities. His studies clarify how critical the personal evaluation of the situation and one's coping options are for stress development.

If stressors cannot be avoided or reduced, at least their impact can be reduced through various coping strategies. For example, by using the previously described relaxation methods or not letting things get that far in the first place and reducing stress from the outset through targeted stress management.

What is preventive stress management?

As the name suggests, preventive stress management is intended to serve as a preventative measure. One can differentiate between primary preventive stress management, secondary preventive stress management, and tertiary preventive stress management in preventive stress management.

Primarily preventive stress management is mainly about helping healthy people to maintain their health and preventing stress so that burnout or the like cannot occur in the first place.

Secondary preventive stress management is about helping people exposed to an increased risk of developing stress-related illnesses due to their professional or personal situation with early detection and prevention.

Tertiary preventive stress management is aimed at people who are already suffering from burnout. It is used to treat and prevent other stress-related illnesses.

What are the goals of preventive stress management?

Through preventive stress management, future stressful situations should be perceived and recognized at an early stage to be reduced in the long term. In this way, the quality of life can be maintained or even increased. Also, the aim is to ensure that there is no impairment of health or severe illnesses in the first place.

The methods and tips already described can help you with this.

Who is preventive stress management suitable for?

In principle, preventive stress management is suitable for everyone because, as already explained, it is about the prevention of stress, no matter how badly you have affected yourself and of no value whether you are already suffering from signs of an illness such as burnout.

Prevent stress through resilience

Resilience is the inner resistance to potentially disease-causing demands or situations. It is the ability to stay healthy despite minor as well as significant stresses.

It is primarily about mobilizing your self-healing powers and building a specific resistance to moments of stress.

It is also about successfully coping with crises - perhaps you can even be seen as an opportunity for development?

Can I learn resilience?

Yes, resilience can be learned. There are, for example, resilience training and coaching that can help to better deal with tension and stress.

To increase one's own ability to resilience, professional stress management, as described above, can help.

Reduce and avoid stress with an excellent work-life balance

A healthy work-life balance is essential, especially in stressful times. This means that work (= work) and leisure time, family, social activities (= life) should be in a balanced relationship to one another. Anyone who has a very stressful job should create a balance so that body and mind can relax and stress can be reduced.

An ideal work-life balance is understood to mean that both areas support each other positively instead of influencing each other.

It is, of course, best if you try not to work too much from the start and create enough space for yourself. Flexible working hours can also help to achieve an excellent work-life balance.

Stress prevention for health: which diseases can you prevent with stress relief?

Chronic stress can make you sick. This is a fact that most people are undoubtedly aware of by now. If the pressure is permanently too high and it is no longer possible to cope with it, it can affect our health. For example, the risk of a heart attack or depression is doubled in chronically stressed people compared to non-stressed people.

The following physical complaints can occur:

- diabetes

- Alzheimer

- increased mortality from cardiovascular diseases

- Autoimmune diseases

- Arrhythmia

- Digestive problems (diarrhoea, gas, nausea)

- Irritable bowel syndrome

- stomach pain

- Stomach ulcers

- Circulatory problems (dizziness)

- Rashes

- Hair loss

- high blood pressure

- Weight gain or weight loss

- increased cholesterol

The following psychological complaints can occur:

- burnout

- depressions

- Exhaustion

Therefore, everyone must find an opportunity for themselves to cope with challenging situations and stress in everyday life without affecting our psyche and our body.

Whether sport, relaxation techniques or small breaks in between - whatever you do to reduce stress, it is essential to do it regularly. It is best to develop a routine so that you can refer to it better in hectic times.

The effects of my years of stress have forced me to take action against the pressure.

When I was in my early 20s, I was still full of energy. There was only one goal, namely to advance professionally. I opened one business at a time and enjoyed being successful. I loved to be stressed, challenged anew every day, and needed by my employees as decision-makers. I didn't even think about relaxation; on the contrary, I asked for the pressure. I wanted to work tirelessly, to get something off the ground successfully.

After a few years, there was disillusionment. The business was worse. I worked longer and longer, but I no longer had the successes I had before. When I got to the office in the morning, I felt panic about the day's chores. Nothing happened fast enough for me, and no employee could do me justice. I became more and more impatient, and my inner restlessness increased. When the stress at work began to manifest itself in physical symptoms, I began to worry.

From then on, I was forced to find something with which I could relax. The method had to work efficiently and reliably. Above all else, it had to be quick to apply because I had little time available. In my search, I came across psycho-cybernetics: the control and regulation between consciousness and body.

Over the years, I have become an "expert" in managing stress in other methods as well.

My first seminars showed me that there were consistently positive results. It is now a matter of personal concern to me to pass on my experiences and lessons from the last 18 years to those around me who are stressed out.

Chapter 10 My personal story.

How did it start?

I left this part to the end because I know as a former anxious person that reading an anxious anecdote can make other people uneasy.

As with every story, this one starts at the beginning. But as we talk about anxiety and panic, it always starts a few months earlier with an upside-down sleeping schedule, bad feelings, and a bad environment, negative thoughts and possibly a bad or toxic relationship. It all started roughly 8 years ago whilst I was still living in Hungary. I still used to lived in Hungary at that time. It started roughly about 8 years ago. So I believe I must have been on the edge of a panic attack several times, but I always just disregard the feeling and went on with my day. I had this kind of pre-panic level of fear before fights or during very bad arguments, but I've never gone over that edge. Well, there was a day when I did not stay in my safe state of mind. I went to my local pub, as one does on a cozy afternoon, had a good chat with my friends and had a soft drink in the afternoon as it was mid-week

I did not drink alcohol. I was about to leave, another friend came in and said:

"C'mon man, are you about to leave just now?"

"Well, I have work tomorrow" I replied.

"Don't be like this! Have a drink with us then you can go! "

So I said "yeah.. okay… one beer." (I didn't need a lot of persuasion)

The next day I woke up at the bus station, I must have blacked out as I had no idea what happened. I suppose somebody may have put something in my drink. The last thing I remember was that one beer. It wasn't a close friend. He was the kind of guy who would come to the pub every now and then and try to find good company for a chat and some drinks.

Suddenly my phone rang. I picked it up.

"Who is there?"

"Who do you think? Your boss." he replied. "Where are you? We are already late!"

So I told him, they picked me up, and we were on our way to the capital. Whilst we were in the van and on the way out of the city I started to feel that I couldn't breathe. I disregarded the feeling as 'yeah, whatever, I will probably have 2 packs of cigarettes done by the end of the night if I feel like this.'

Suddenly I felt like my body was just not taking in any oxygen, my limbs felt numb, I started hyperventilating, my heart felt like somebody had pushed a dagger through it. I remember thinking to myself 'Hmm, so this is how I'm gonna die, after a drunken party night, and I don't even remember if I managed to score with somebody.' I just shouted "pull over. I need to get out of the van right now." We stopped, then I opened my door and fell out onto the grass like a sack of potatos. My whole body was limp, and I could not breathe. The task to pick me up required 2 people, not because I was heavy but because I was like a ragdoll.

My boss at that time had had 3 heart attacks, so he thought that I was having one right now. They immediately put me back into the van and drove to the nearest hospital. Got me from both sides and carried me into the emergency room. Luckily nobody was waiting there, so they took me in in a matter of minutes but first they wanted me to sign a paper. Well, that was the most challenging signature of my life. My hands were shaking so badly, and my mind could not put together the spelling, so I just shouted "Just take me in, Ma'am, I'm gonna die right now, I'll sign later if I survive. If not, my parents will!"

My colleagues just laughed, and the nurse showed the way to the emergency room. They took a blood sample to check if I was under the influence of alcohol or any other substances. Well, I knew for a fact that I was not.. I was at that time living a rigorous sporty lifestyle, so an occasional beer and nicotine was the most severe substance I would have taken. Then the nurse came back with the results from the lab, she said "yeah, we better call the police. You have quite a mixture of things here."

I was about to pass out, they gave me some sedatives to calm down. I explained to the doctor with a confident muttering that I would not take any drugs as I have exercised 5-6 times a week, so I can't afford to spend my time or health on something mediocre like that.

He just nodded.

When I was steady on my legs, they finally sent me to another part of the hospital to a psychologist. He explained that I have an anxiety disorder, and that what I had experienced was a panic attack. I told him "Nah, mate, that only happens with weak-minded people." He replied "No it can happen to anybody in any age, gender"

He further explained that it's gonna stay with me for life, and I have to take medicine to 'keep me sane for the time being', or else when it gets worse, to take the edge off. So I took medication. Thanked him for his help and went home.

The first weeks after the 'event'

The following weeks I barely left my Aunt's flat.

Going to the shop was even too much of a stress, so generally, anything could have pushed me over the edge. My mind was in pieces.

I did decide not to take medicine, just meditate, relax, get over it. Those things did help for a bit, but I was inconsistent and carried on with some of my more destructive habits, still staying up very late. I still fell asleep watching films, and still woke up with my phone in my hands accompanied with 2 coffees. I've slept 4-5 hours on average and my general way of living was kind of a mess. I needed to stop my exercises. Whenever my heart rate went up, I started to crumble down into a thick pile of a sorry excuse of a man. So, from 74kgs (163.1 pounds), I rapidly went down to 62kgs (136 pounds). I felt incredibly sorry for myself, and I did not take any of the help they would have provided me at the hospital. I was looking at the mirror every day and saw a stranger staring back at me. A skinny weak man who can't even go to the shop or meet up with friends. Eventually I was kicked out of my job as I was unable to attend to do any kind of work. The mere idea of being stuck in a van for hours made me terrified. After that, I had about 2 months off until I got myself together enough to move to my own place and look for another job. My family was pushing me to 'just get over it already'.

I'm not blaming them by any means, for them it was an unknown territory, so it was for me too.

The panic and anxiety, in general, was my sidekick, on and off for the following 8 years, sometimes no symptoms at all for months, sometimes all symptoms for months. The last time it came back, I decided that I should put an end to this story because I can't possibly live my life like this.

Luckily I'm not the kind of person who would turn against himself by the means of suicide. I needed a serious change.

The solution

I decided to look over how my life got to this point. I worked hard from month to month and developed my new way of living and thinking to finally eliminate this horrible state of mind.

I put together a 'To-do list' so I can track my progress. I didn't set big goals at first, just small steps and things that are easily doable every day. Whenever I finished something on the list it was just pure blessing, and it continued to motivate me. Then as I progressed forward I did put bigger and bigger but still achievable tasks on the list to further motivate myself.

First of all I put together a sleeping schedule, recognised my triggers and went easy on myself with stress and self-judgement. I have made the agreement with myself to commit to the cause and not let anything stand in my way to get back to where I was, and get even better than I was before my first panic attack.

Secondly I worked out how to get over the panic feeling once I'm already falling into that anxious state.

Then I focused on my diet, improving the quality of it and stopped eating right after waking up and right before I went to sleep. (I do leave a gap of around 1.5 hours minimum)

I've put a stop to social media usage in the morning.

There is absolutely no need for swiping the social media platforms during your first waking hours. Taking care of your own mind and body is far more important.

I eliminated the processed foods from my diet and introduced more raw vegetables and fruit into it.

I reduced sugar intake altogether.

I always drink my water.

Being hydrated reduces anxiety and your mind and body is works far better.

To calculate how much water you need is easy, you just count 50 milliliters per kg of your body weight. I'm around 70kgs now so i drink 3-3.5 liters per day.

I started to leave out coffee from my morning routine and delayed my first coffee until 9 or 10am when I was already well awake and I knew it wouldn't affect me anymore. If caffeine gives you the jitters then you can leave it out all together, it's not a necessity.

I began to be grateful about everything good that's happening to me, everything I accomplish, everybody around me who is trying to help and even for my naysayers who tried to hold me back, yes for them too. Naysayers especially can be your best motivation for they can't see the big picture you are moving towards and they can't comprehend the struggle but they'll see the results as you come back from that abyss to previously unknown heights victorious. The more grateful I became, the more positivity got caught in my net.

I filled my mind with positive thoughts and whenever I needed to do a task or to do simple steps to get closer to my success I rephrased my negative thoughts regarding the task or a person.

I pulled towards positive people and towards people who are more successful than me, more intelligent than me because as I saw beforehand, they tend to pull you along with them on their journey.

I implemented the 60 second rule into my everyday life.

If a task takes less than or up to 60 seconds I'm not gonna sit on it, I'll do it immediately. Wash the dishes right after eating? Yes I do it now! Pick up my laundry and chuck it into the washing machine? Yes I'll do it now! The list just goes on with everything else that can be accomplished in 60 seconds.

I do yoga whenever I can squeeze it into my daily schedule. Usually it's not easy because I'm always busy but I'm not making excuses to myself as it would just pull me back and now I'm turning my face towards goals, none of my intentions involve going back to square one.

Conclusion

Now I'm just following these simple steps in my everyday life and feel grateful for this decision every day.

If I need to write my own list, what have I accomplished in the last few years? Well, pretty steep learning curve right there:

- Learned 2 new languages
- started a new life in a different country
- visited 4 new countries and over 160 new cities (Google say so)
- have a fantastic relationship
- I have found great people and amazing friends along my journey
- I'm happy every day
- I reduced my social media usage to a minimum
- I'm sleeping well
- I wake up happy every day

- I'm grateful for everything that comes my way and the list goes on and on and on endlessly.

Endnote!

I'm glad you made it to the end, and as you did, I believe you are on your way to being happier and more mindful! If you liked my work, consider leaving positive or negative feedback on Amazon. That would help my work, and it will help to make it possible to publish my upcoming books! Thank you for being here, and I wish you the best!